Advance Praise

"As an amateur woodworker, I can state from experience that there's nothing like having the right tools for the job you're trying to do. Here Andy Thomson and Clare Aukofer have assembled an oh-so-handy tool chest for the layperson who wants to think more clearly about the ever-less-mystical origins of religious belief."
—August E. Brunsman IV, Executive Director, Secular Student Alliance

"Simply put, this book provides the most compelling scientific explanation for religion ever advanced. Andy Thomson and Clare Aukofer explicate precisely that evolved psychological and brain mechanisms combine to produce religious experiences, and show how religious leaders exploit these mechanisms, sometimes with disastrous results. The book is fascinating from start to finish. It's at the top of my 'most highly recommended books' for 2011."
—David M. Buss, author of *Evolutionary Psychology: The New Science of the Mind*

"Despite all the advancements we have made in science, technology, and medicine, our Paleolithic psychology continues to drag us down into the abyss of archaic beliefs, blind faith, and tribal conflict. Andy Thomson and Clare Aukofer explain to us not only why the human mind is so susceptible to believing the unbelievable but also why we are willing to not only die for it, but kill for it as well. Read this book, and when you are done—send it to your congressional representative."
—R. Elisabeth Cornwell, PhD, Executive Director, Richard Dawkins Foundation for Reason and Science

"As Andy Thomson and Clare Aukofer point out in this compelling little book, our snap judgments are 'millions of years in the making' and so is the human propensity to construct and to believe in gods. I know of no clearer or more concise summary of the various preadaptations that cause us to generate and sustain religious belief."
—Sarah B. Hrdy, author of *I⁣ ⁣ ⁣: The Evolutionary Origins of Mutuⁱ*

"In my life I've seen how desperately we need rational thinking in public policy. This book, dealing with the ultimate issues, can be a framework guiding us to a more rational worldview."
—Sean Faircloth, Executive Director, Secular Coalition for America

"How does the human brain generate belief in an invisible god? Spurred by his study of suicide terrorism, psychiatrist Andy Thomson and Clare Aukofer elegantly describe many innate capacities of the human brain to explain how we can believe in an unknowable phenomenon: god. The writing is clear, fair, deeply knowledgeable, wickedly intelligent, and full of new scientific facts about how the mind works. This topic touches all of us, from those who wait to pass through airport security to those who live under religious tyranny. Know thy neighbor and thyself; Thomson and Aukofer have given us a smart read."
—Helen Fisher, PhD, Biological Anthropologist, Rutgers University, and author of *Why Him? Why Her?*

"Brain washed? Andy Thomson and Clare Aukofer clearly explain why we are so susceptible to religious belief. Priests, rabbis, and imams ask us to dance, and then seduce us—and it appears we have a hardwired vulnerability to the seduction. *Why We Believe in God(s)* is easy and fun to read (and it's got pictures). No wonder so much of the world believes the fairy tales."
—Woody Kaplan, Chair, Advisory Board of the Secular Coalition for America, and President, Defending Dissent Foundation

"A much-needed summary of current research on a fascinating question. Many theists ask how religion could be so pervasive if it isn't true, and this book provides a collection of answers."
—Amanda K. Metskas, Executive Director, Camp Quest, Inc.

"A stimulating and enlightening journey into the mind we all possess, a mind primed to believe. Andy Thomson and Clare Aukofer take us on a fast-paced trek from how the human brain evolved in a primitive world to how religion harnesses those adaptations in the modern world."
—Todd Stiefel, President, Stiefel Freethought Foundation

why we believe in god(s)

A Concise Guide to the Science of Faith

J. Anderson Thomson, Jr., MD
with Clare Aukofer

Foreword by Richard Dawkins

PITCHSTONE PUBLISHING
Charlottesville, Virginia

Pitchstone Publishing
Charlottesville, Virginia 22901

18 17 16 15 14 13 12 11   1 2 3 4 5

Library of Congress Cataloging-in-Publication Data

Thomson, J. Anderson.
    Why we believe in god(s) : a concise guide to the science of faith / J.
Anderson Thomson, Jr. with Clare Aukofer ; [foreword by Richard Dawkins].
        p. cm.
    Includes bibliographical references.
    ISBN 978-0-9844932-1-0 (pbk. : alk. paper)
  1. Psychology, Religious. 2. Faith—Psychology. 3. Religion and science. I.
Aukofer, Clare. II. Title.
    BL53.T46 2011
    200.1'9—dc22
                                                                    2010053504

For Jack,
my grandson,
in the hopes that he will grow up in a world
freer of religion's destructiveness

Contents

Plates

Foreword by Richard Dawkins

In one of the great understatements of history, *The Origin of Species* confines its discussion of human evolution to a laconic prophecy: "Light will be thrown on the origin of man and his history." Less often quoted is the beginning of the same paragraph: "In the distant future I see open fields for far more important researches. Psychology will be based on a new foundation." Dr. Thomson is one of the evolutionary psychologists now making Darwin's forecast come true, and this book about the evolutionary drivers of religiosity would have delighted the old man.

Darwin, though not religious in his maturity, understood the religious impulse. He was a benefactor of Down church and he regularly walked his family there on Sundays (then continued his walk while they went inside). He had been trained to the life of a clergyman, and William Paley's *Natural Theology* was his favored undergraduate reading. Darwin killed natural theology's *answer* stone dead, but he never lost his preoccupation with its *question*: the question of function. It is no surprise that he was intrigued by the functional question of religiosity. Why do most people, and all peoples, harbor religious beliefs? "Why" is to be understood in the special functional sense that we today, though not Darwin himself, would call "Darwinian."

How, to put the Darwinian question in modern terms, does religiosity contribute to the survival of genes promoting it? Thomson is a leading proponent of the "by-product" school of thought: religion itself need have no survival value; it is a *by-product* of psychological predispositions that have.

"Fast food" is a *leitmotif* of the book: "if you understand the psychology of fast food, you understand the psychology of religion." Sugar is another good example. It was impossible for our wild ancestors to get enough of it, so we have inherited an open-ended craving that, now that it is easily met, damages our health.

> These fast-food cravings are a by-product. And now they become dangerous, because, uncontrolled, they can lead to health problems our ancestors likely never faced. . . . Which brings us to religion.

Another leading evolutionary psychologist, Steven Pinker, explains our love of music in a similar "by-product" way, as "auditory cheesecake, an exquisite confection crafted to tickle the sensitive spots of at least six of our mental faculties." For Pinker, the mental faculties supernormally tickled as a by-product by music are mostly concerned with the sophisticated brain software required to disentangle meaningful sounds (for example, language) from background bedlam.

Thomson's fast-food theory of religion emphasizes, rather, those psychological predispositions that can be called *social*: "adaptive psychological mechanisms that evolved to help us negotiate our relationships with other people, to detect agency and intent, and to generate a sense of safety. These mechanisms were forged in the not-so-distant world of our African homeland."

Thomson's chapters identify a series of evolved mental faculties exploited by religion, each one beguilingly labelled with a line familiar from scripture or liturgy: "Our Daily Bread", "Deliver Us from Evil", "Thy Will Be Done", "Lest Ye Be Judged." There are some compelling images:

> Think of a two-year-old child reaching out to be picked up and cuddled. He extends his hands above his head and beseeches you. Think now of the Pentecostal worshipper who speaks in tongues. He stretches out his hands above his head, beseeching god in the same "pick-me-up-and-hold-me" gesture. We may lose human attachment figures through death, through misunderstandings, through distance, but a god is always there for us.

To most of us, that arms-extended gesture of the worshipper looks merely foolish. After reading Thomson we shall see it through more penetrating eyes: it is not just foolish, it is infantile.

Then there is our eagerness to detect the deliberate hand of agency.

Why is it you mistake a shadow for a burglar but never a burglar for a shadow? If you hear a door slam, why do you wonder who did it before you consider the wind as the culprit? Why might a child who sees blowing tree limbs through a window fear that it's the boogeyman come to get him?

The hyperactive agency detection device evolved in the brains of our wild ancestors because of a risk asymmetry. A rustle in the long grass is statistically more likely to be the wind than a leopard. But the cost of a mistake is higher one way than the other. Agents, like leopards and burglars, can kill. Best go with the statistically unlikely guess. (Darwin himself made the point, in an anecdote about his dog's response to a wind-blown parasol.) Thomson pursues the thought—oversensitivity to *agents* where there are none—and gives us his elegant explanation of another of the psychological biases upon which religiosity is founded.

Our Darwinian preoccupation with kinship is yet another. For example, in Roman Catholic lore,

The nuns are "sisters" or even "mother superiors," the priests are "fathers," the monks are "brothers," the Pope is the "Holy Father," and the religion itself is referred to as the "Holy Mother Church."

Dr. Thomson has made a special study of suicide bombers, and he notes how kin-based psychology is exploited in their recruitment and training:

Charismatic recruiters and trainers create cells of fictive kin, pseudobrothers outraged at the treatment of their Muslim brothers and sisters and separated from actual kin. The appeal of such martyrdom is not just the sexual fantasy of multiple heavenly virgins, but the chance to give chosen kin punched tickets to paradise.

One by one, the other components of religion—community worship, obedience to priestly authority, ritual—receive the Thomson treatment. Every point he makes has the ring of truth, abetted by a crisp style and vivid imagery. Andy Thomson is an outstandingly persuasive lecturer, and it shines through his writing. This short, punchy book will be swiftly read—and long remembered.

Preface

This book arose as an echo of 9/11. My son, Matthew, was training for a new job in a building next to the World Trade Center; he witnessed firsthand the nightmare. My response to his brush with death was to study suicide terrorism.

I am no stranger to human destructiveness. My profession as a forensic psychiatrist gives me in-depth contact with violent men. And for many years I was part of the Center for the Study of Mind and Human Interaction at the University of Virginia, a unique interdisciplinary group of mental health professionals, diplomats, and historians founded by psychiatrist Vamık Volkan that traveled to hot spots throughout the world to study and mediate intense conflict.

But despite my professional work and experience with traumatized societies, in the course of my study of suicide terrorism I discovered a largely new and ever-expanding world of ideas and evidence about the human mind, specifically as it relates to religion. The books and articles I utilized were academic, some more accessible than others. I discovered there was no single source that laid out these exciting new ideas in a way easily accessible to an interested reader. That is what I've tried to do here.

Religion never made much sense to me. But, like most dutiful sons, I went along with my elders' beliefs. If it seemed right to them, the people I admired and respected, who knew the world and life, then I best join the procession. Even though I said I believed, there was little emotional conviction to those beliefs. Singing in the choir with my buddies provided pleasant time with friends on Wednesday evenings and Sunday mornings. Though the Presbyterian hymnal we used seemed like a collection of funeral dirges, good religious music can be spectacular. Handel's *Messiah* moves me to this day.

My training as a psychoanalytically oriented psychiatrist exposed me to Sigmund Freud's *The Future of an Illusion*, and Freud certainly contributed to our understanding of why human minds generate religious beliefs. Yet, his is far from a complete explanation.

Already steeped in the new discipline of evolutionary psychology, I found, in my research on suicide terrorism, the work of such scholars as Scott Atran, Jesse Bering, Pascal Boyer, Stuart Guthrie, Richard Sosis, and Lee Kirkpatrick a revelation. They had figured out religion—or were damn close. Their work informed my three-pronged analysis of suicide bombers.

A bare-bones formulation of suicide terrorism, supported by the evidence, reads as follows: male-bonded coalitionary violence, with lethal raiding against innocents, is as old as our species, even older. That capacity is embedded in all males. The potential for suicide resides in all of us, both male and female. The evidence suggests two types of evolved suicide potentials: negative inclusive fitness and retaliation bargaining. The first arises from a sense of burdensomeness and animates female suicide bombers, such as widows or outcasts. The second characterizes male suicide bombers and originates from positions of humiliation and powerlessness. Because religion is a cultural construct, a product of human minds, many of the evolved cognitive adaptations that generate religious beliefs can be exploited to motivate suicide terrorism. This makes religion an astoundingly powerful ideology that can simultaneously hijack the evolved capacities for both lethal raiding and suicide. It all fit together.

Publication of that analysis, aided by Clare Aukofer, and presentations of my suicide-terrorism formulation kept my focus on religion. Reviewer and audience responses expanded my ideas.

By early 2009 I had combined my research and developed a one-hour presentation to explain why we believe in god(s). Thanks to Richard Dawkins and his foundation, the Richard Dawkins Foundation for Reason and Science, the presentation was superbly filmed, edited, and posted on YouTube, where it drew hundreds of thousands of views in a brief span of time. That level of interest told me that there might be widespread interest in a brief, clear, and concise guide to the new science of religion, and that became the genesis of this book.

Clare Aukofer worked her magic on my prose, provided invaluable extensions and examples for many of the ideas, and had the inspired idea to utilize the astounding NASA image of the Helix nebula, the so-called Eye of God, partly photographed using the Hubble telescope. All authors should be blessed with such a colleague.

My aim is to have the reader quickly up to speed. Within the brief time it takes for you to read this slim volume, you should be able to grasp how the mind and brain work to generate and sustain religious belief. (And if you have questions, I welcome your correspondence.)

Finish the book. Refer to it often. Give it to a friend. Donate it to a library or school. We now know why and how our minds manufacture and spread beliefs in god(s), and new research continues to add on to what we know. This knowledge can free us. Anything we can do, no matter how small, to loosen fundamentalist religion's grasp on humanity strikes a blow for civilization and boosts the chances for a truly global civil society—and perhaps even for our species' long-term survival. If you're religious, and you've picked up this book, it's probably for a reason. So read on.

Acknowledgments

Richard Dawkins deserves special thanks for his kind foreword to this book, for his work, and for giving me the opportunity to serve as a trustee with the Richard Dawkins Foundation for Reason and Science. Knowing him and working with his foundation have been an immeasurable privilege. A portion of the royalties from the sale of this book are assigned to the foundation. If you purchased this book, you made a donation to the foundation. Thank you.

I will always be deeply grateful to Robin Elisabeth Cornwell, the executive director of the Richard Dawkins Foundation for Reason and Science. She has been a great friend and colleague in this work. She gave earlier versions of this book careful scrutiny and assistance and provided me with unparalleled opportunities to present my ideas to audiences around the country.

My fellow trustees at the Foundation, Greg Langer and Todd Stiefel, reviewed earlier versions of the manuscript and have been great supporters of this endeavor.

Our publisher, Kurt Volkan, deserves high praise for his enthusiasm from the first moments of our collaboration and his wise editing and guidance throughout the process.

Willis Spaulding opened the doors for me to evolutionary psychology with his gift of Robert Wright's *The Moral Animal*. His son Tristan gave the book's first draft an invaluable critique.

Scott Atran, Justin Barrett, Jesse Bering, Paul Bloom, Pascal Boyer, Stewart Guthrie, Lee Kirkpatrick, and Richard Sosis stand out among the researchers who have discerned the cognitive architecture of religion.

Paul Andrews, Martin Brüne, David Buss, Joe Carroll, Leda Cosmides, Martin Daly, Robin Dunbar, Josh Duntley, Anne Eisen, A. J. Figueredo, Helen Fisher, Russ Gardner, Edward Hagen, Sarah Hrdy, Owen Jones, Rob Kurzban, Geoffrey Miller, Randy Nesse, Craig Palmer, Steven Pinker, John Richer, Nancy Segal, Todd Shackelford, Wulf Schiefenhevel, Frank Sulloway, Randy Thornhill, John Tooby, Paul Watson, Carol and Glenn Weisfeld, Andreas Wilke, and all those involved in evolutionary psychology and human ethology have enriched my thinking beyond measure through their writings and my conversations with them each year at the annual meeting of the Human Behavior and Evolution Society and the biannual meetings of the International Society for Human Ethology. I miss Linda Mealey, John Pearce, and Margo Wilson, who warmly welcomed a neophyte and are no longer with us.

Although he will disagree with me on some of the views in this book, I am most grateful to my University of Virginia colleague Jonathan Haidt, who guided my thinking on the psychology of morality.

Many of my psychiatrist friends and colleagues have helped with articles or by challenging my thinking on religion, especially Salman Akhtar, Ira Brenner, and Bruce Greyson. Salman and the Margaret Mahler Foundation invited me to present at the annual Mahler Symposium in Philadelphia and the chapter in the volume of those papers is the first time my attempt at synthesis of the by-product theory of religion saw print. My mentor Vamık Volkan gave me an opportunity to work at his unique center at the University of Virginia, work that took me to traumatized and conflict-ridden societies throughout the world. He also coedited a volume on terrorism that included my first article with my formulation of suicide terrorism.

Hawes Spencer, editor of *The Hook*, in Charlottesville, Virginia, published my article on suicide terrorism for a general audience. The piece, which Clare Aukofer and Rosalind Warfield-Brown had polished, generated controversy due to the ideas on religion also found in this book.

Jim Simmonds supplied me with crucial books and articles. Miles Townsend questions everything, thank god(s). Russ Federman, the senior author on a book I wrote with him for young adults with bipolar illness, gave me the confidence to do this book. June Cleveland, my irreplaceable forensic secretary, typed the first draft of this book.

William "Bill" Ober, my medical school classmate, has been a biology textbook and medical illustrator extraordinaire since I have known him. His drawings will help the reader see how religion originates in our brains.

Richard Potts, the director of the Human Origins Program at the Smithsonian Institute's National Museum of Natural History in Washington, DC, reviewed the book's summary of human evolution. If you have not yet visited the museum's magnificent Hall of Human Origins, do so soon.

Michael Persinger kindly checked my summary of his brilliant work with the "God Helmet."

Amanda Metskas and August Brunsman gave the final draft a rich and useful critique.

American Atheists, Atheist Alliance International, Virginia Atheists and Agnostics, New York City Atheists, Atheists United of Los Angeles, Western State Hospital in Staunton, Virginia, and the Secular Student Alliance at George Washington University, George Mason University, and Carnegie Mellon University have all heard talks with this material. I so appreciate the opportunities and their questions and suggestions.

Ayaan Hirsi Ali and the Four Horsemen—Richard Dawkins, Daniel Dennett, Sam Harris, and Christopher Hitchens—hold a special place in my heart for their writings, their debates with believers, and their fierce courage when they give religion and its apologists no diplomatic free pass.

This work has been a labor of love, love for the science and admiration for the scientists who map the mind's religion-making mechanisms. If I have made their ideas shine for you, thank them. Where there are errors, take me to task.

A. HUMAN BRAIN, LATERAL VIEW

Lateral cortex.
Perception of self and others'
bodies. Physical attributes.

Parietal lobe.

Temporal lobe.

Amygdala. Fear.

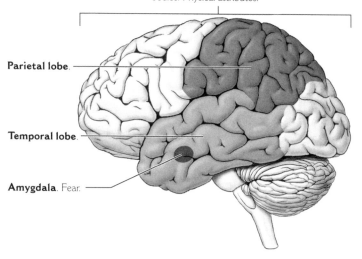

B. HUMAN BRAIN, MIDSAGITTAL VIEW

Medial frontal cortex.
Perceptions of self and
others' emotions, desires,
beliefs and intentions.

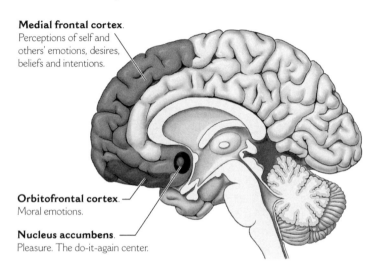

Orbitofrontal cortex.
Moral emotions.

Nucleus accumbens.
Pleasure. The do-it-again center.

why we believe in god(s)

1

In the Beginning Was the Word
Our Propensity to Believe

It is not the strongest of the species that survives, nor the most intelligent. . . . It is the one that is the most adaptable to change.

—Charles Darwin

There are those who say that evolution conflicts with faith, or that the natural wonders of evolution were kick-started by some sort of sentient, omniscient being. Yet if an all-powerful, all-seeing god does exist, he designed into the creation and evolution of man something powerful: the propensity to believe in a god.

Throughout recorded history, from the ancient Egyptians to the Aztecs to the Romans and beyond—Polytheist, Christian, Jew, Muslim, Hindu, Buddhist, Pagan, Satanist, Scientologist—all known cultures have revolved around some concept of at least one god and/or central mystical figure, with or without a corresponding supernatural world. Why? Why is religion an apparently universal feature of humans and the cultures we create?

We are beginning to understand. Over the past two decades there has been a revolution in psychology and the cognitive neurosciences. Out of it has come an evolutionary explanation of why human minds generate religious belief, why we generate specific types of beliefs, and why our minds are prone to accept and spread them.

We now have robust theories with empirical evidence, including evidence from imaging studies—pictures of the brain itself—that supports these explanations. The pieces are in place; we can now look to science for a comprehensive understanding of why human minds produce and accept religious ideas and why humans will alter their behavior for, die for, and kill for these ideas.

Charles Darwin's theory of natural selection remains one of the most important ideas that ever occurred to a human mind, and the evidence proves him right. Natural selection is the sole workable scientific explanation for the variety and design of all life—plant, animal, and every other form—on this earth. It is also the only workable explanation for the design and function of the human mind, which is the real birthplace of gods.

Look around. We are all the same species, *Homo sapiens*. Yet we come in all shapes and sizes and with varying capacities. But for all the variation, many traits are heritable. We tend to resemble our parents and close kin, sharing strengths and weaknesses with those ancestors who came before. We are all descendents of success.

The term "survival of the fittest" is often misunderstood. In the Darwinian sense, fitness is the ability to adapt, to survive, and to reproductively thrive. The struggle for survival winnows out organisms lacking that ability.

Of course, Darwin did not have the advantage of knowing precisely how traits passed from one generation to the next. That had to wait until 1953, when James Watson and Francis Crick unraveled the structure of DNA, and in so doing instantly saw its possible copying mechanism and identified the means of inheritance.

Combining Darwin with Watson and Crick, natural selection with genetics, creates the modern Darwinian synthesis. To survive, we adapt over evolutionary time, just as Darwin's Galapagos creatures adapted to their unique environments. Nowhere else do iguanas live in the ocean, the obvious solution to the problem of finding food and surviving on a tiny island. Even from island to island, each with its own isolated ecosystem, creatures in the Galapagos faced slightly different problems and solved them differently. They adapted. But more importantly, they passed those adaptations on.

Every organism, including the human one, is an integrated collection of adaptations—problem-solving devices—shaped by natural selection over the vast stretches of evolutionary time. Each adaptation promotes in some specific way the survival of the genes that directed the construction of those adaptations.

At every level, from molecules to minds, we see Darwinian natural selection at work.

Look at yourself. To survive, you need oxygen. As a developing organism, you needed to evolve a way to efficiently extract the oxygen from the air and distribute it throughout your body.

The structure of your heart solves the survival problem of pumping blood. The protein hemoglobin solves the problem of transporting oxygen to our brain and other organs. The oxygen in the hemoglobin pumped by the heart comes from lungs that solve the problem of extracting oxygen from the air. And so on. We simply call that whole process "breathing."

This modern synthesis applies also to the human mind and the human brain. The brain is an organ, and as Harvard psychologist and researcher Steven Pinker notes, the mind is what the brain does. And the brain, like every other piece of living tissue, is an elegantly integrated collection of devices designed through natural selection to solve specific problems of survival over vast stretches of evolutionary time. These adaptations, including social adaptations that helped us survive in small groups, evolved within the brain to promote in some way the continuation of the genes that directed their construction.

When you look at a face, the image on your retina actually is upside down and two dimensional. Your brain converts that image into an upright three-dimensional face using a myriad of visual adaptations: color detectors, motion detectors, shape detectors, edge detectors—all working symbiotically, silently, and seamlessly.

Our ancestors evolved a myriad of equally complex social adaptations. When you see that face, you also make abstract judgments about sex, age, attractiveness, status, emotional state, personality, and the contents of that individual's unseen mind, including intentions, beliefs, and desires. These judgment-forming adaptations are largely outside of awareness, many forever unconscious. Your snap judgments are millions of years in the making.

The mind/brain is relentlessly complex. Consider the Apollo spacecraft, a packed array of engineering devices, each dedicated to analyzing a constant stream of information and solving a particular problem, all while the astronauts are consciously aware of only a select few. We work the same way. Consider all of the things you are conscious of; they are a very small part of an entire system, the tip of the iceberg of what goes on in your mind.

This is important to understand because religion, while not an adaptation in itself, derives from the same mind-brain social adaptations that we use to navigate the sea of people who surround us. These adaptations formed to solve specific social and interpersonal problems as humanity evolved. Almost incidentally, but no less powerfully, they come together to construct the foundation of every religious idea, belief, and ritual. Religious beliefs are basic human social survival concepts with slight alterations.

That religion is a by-product of adaptations that occurred for other reasons does not negate its incredible power. As we'll explain in chapter 9, reading and writing are not in themselves adaptations; they also are by-products of adaptations designed for other purposes.

All religions—as sets of beliefs concerning the cause, nature, and purpose of the universe—begin with belief in one or more central holy figures or teachers. Most also involve a deity or deities capable of interacting with us, able and willing to intervene in our lives, to hear our silent wishes, and to grant them, and capable of doing literally anything. For our purposes, we'll discuss just one, and designate it as male, though some religions have multiples with differing powers and a few have snuck in female personalities. Still, they are all remarkably similar. Certainly the god of the three major Abrahamic religions is the same, so we'll use "him" for our examples.

That god is paternal and, like a good father, loves us unconditionally. Usually, though, he only hears our prayers if we worship him hard enough, make sacrifices of some sort, acknowledge that we are highly imperfect and thank him profusely (whether or not he grants our wishes), and believe that we are all born bad. This god makes decisions based on not only our prayers but also the prayers of every other human being, or at least every other human being who shares the particulars of our beliefs. Even when he refuses our wishes or needs, we continue to believe that whatever occurs is in our best interests, even if it doesn't seem that way, and that this invisible god has a purpose for everything. And all of this goes in our mind even when we're not thinking about it.

If, when you were a teenager, your mother had set you up on a blind date and assured you that your date was extraordinarily good looking, wealthy beyond measure, kind, loving, willing to do anything for you even though you'd never met, and wanted nothing more than for you to have the best of everything, would you have believed her? Well, maybe when you were a teenager. For a few minutes.

So why are we so willing to believe in an invisible god that does all of that, and more?

Compared to what really goes on in our minds, the concept of one holy supernormal entity seems easy. Just to believe in a god, our mind bounces off of no fewer than twenty hardwired adaptations evolved over eons of natural selection to help us coexist and communicate with our fellow *Homo sapiens* to survive and dominate the planet. In the pages that follow, we'll show you exactly how and why human minds not only accept the impossible but also have created cults of it.

We will show you how and why humans came to, among other things, believe in a god, love a god, fear a god, defer to a god, envision a god like us, pray to a god and assume prayers would be answered, create rituals to worship a god, and even die and kill for a god. And we will show you why these hardwired social traits make it extraordinarily difficult to depart from those beliefs, even if and when you are so inclined.

But let's start with a crash course in evolution.

2

In the Image and Likeness
Evolution 101

To kill an error is as good a service as, and sometimes even better than, the establishing of a new truth or fact.

—Charles Darwin

We are risen apes, not fallen angels—and we now have the evidence to prove it. Our vanity might make it difficult to accept, and those who believe in divine creation find the whole concept outrageous. The mere contemplation that humanity could have developed from the "lower" animals has caused many to reject evolution outright, from the moment Charles Darwin promulgated his theory. But the evidence overwhelmingly shows that we evolved along with all other living things from the primordial ooze, where life on earth really began.

Along the east side of the African continent, the Great Rift Valley runs from Ethiopia to Mozambique. Think of this valley as the birth canal of the human species, the true Garden of Eden. This is where our particular species began its unique evolutionary trail.

We did not descend from apes. From a purely scientific viewpoint, we *are* apes. We share 98.6 percent of our DNA with chimpanzees. We also share with them a common ancestor that lived some 5 to 7 million years ago. From that common ancestor, the human line diverged and developed along many different paths, like the varied branches of a bush. Eventually all but one, the one from which you and I evolved, died out.

We are the last surviving example of a specific African ape, the hominid. As evolutionarily recently as 50,000 years ago there may have been four species of closely related but distinct hominids sharing the planet with us. We alone among the hominids survive.

We have now met many of our ancestors. We possess fossils of *Ardipithecus*, probably one of the closest species to the distant ancestor we share with chimps. They seem to have been a pair-bonded species with low levels of aggression.

The *Australopithecus*, meaning the southern ape of Africa, is best known through its most famous fossil, Lucy, found in Ethiopia nearly forty years ago. Fossils of *Paranthropus* (meaning "beside human") found in southern Africa in 1938 and 1948 show it to have had a brain about 40 percent the size of ours; it likely died out because it could not adapt to changes in environment and diet.

In 2008, a nine-year-old boy, the son of a paleontologist, discovered the skull of a considerably older nine-year-old boy in Africa. This skull, also of a hominid since named *Australopithicus sediba*, may provide further links between the australopithecines and us.

Those species, along with our earliest hominid ancestors, coexisted in Africa for about 2 million years, surviving mind-bendingly longer than we have so far.

Our group, *Homo*, shows up in the fossil record about 2 million years ago and includes *Homo habilis*, *Homo erectus*, and *Homo heidelbergensis*. *Homo erectus* made it out of Africa, probably without language, more than a million years ago, migrating as far as the Caucasus Mountains, China, and Indonesia.

It appears that some members of *Homo heidelbergensis* gave rise to the Neanderthals after migrating to Europe, and recent DNA sequencing data suggests that there was some hybridizing between our *Homo sapiens* ancestors and Neanderthals. Those *Homo heidelbergensis* who remained in Africa ultimately gave rise to early, anatomically modern *Homo sapiens*.

The earliest recognized fossils of *Homo sapiens* occur back to nearly 200,000 years ago. There is evidence of symbolic abilities, such as pigments potentially used in coloring, and also evidence of long-distance exchanges and trade between groups, which required a sophisticated means of symbolic communication. It seems likely that the oldest known members of our species probably had the most significant species-specific cognitive, social, and behavioral feature—the ability for language.

You and I, modern *Homo sapiens* with our ability for language, began to leave Africa 60,000 years ago, a blink of the eye in evolutionary time.

Put aside our ethnic, racial, nationalistic, and religious differences. Underneath our skins we are all Africans, the sons and daughters of a small group of hunter-gatherers who arose in Africa, outsurvived all others, and conquered the world.

What is even more amazing is that a severe climate variation between 70,000 and 100,000 years ago apparently reduced our population to perhaps as few as 600 breeding individuals. That is what modern genetics now tells us. That means that every one of the 7 billion people on this planet is a descendant of that small group of hunter-gatherers who lived in Africa and survived the harsh climate change.

Why us? How and why did *we* survive? Comparing *Australopithecus*, *Homo erectus*, and modern human skulls shows a gradual transformation in the area above the eyes. The forehead loses its steep slope and becomes rounded. A brain size of 400 to 500 cubic centimeters in *Australopithecus* doubles for *Homo erectus* and almost triples by the time of modern *Homo sapiens*. That change is particularly notable in the frontal lobe regions. These are the areas of our brain that contain the complex machinery, the evolved adaptations that enable us to negotiate our social worlds.

So what drove the evolution of these big brains of ours? We did. Or, more specifically, others of our species did, because we needed to work together to survive. Physical survival required social survival; we developed "groupishness."

If you arbitrarily divide a room full of people into two groups for a game, they will invariably begin to identify with the group to which they've been assigned. They will consider those in their group as "in," and those in the other as "out." There likely will be strong competition between the two groups, even if the people in them were strangers to each other when the game began. The strangers have become teammates. Hasn't that ever struck you as odd? Probably not, because it is quite literally natural. You most likely would do the same thing. This "groupishness" is hardwired and helped our ancestors survive the worlds in which they evolved.

The crucible of small, tightly knit bands of kin sculpted us into the people we are today. This is not ancient history. As recently as five hundred years ago, two-thirds of the world's population still lived in small hunter-gatherer tribes, the kind of social environment that shaped us and to which we are adapted. In many ways we are still quite tribal in our psychology. But then we are still very young.

So, you ask, what does this have to do with religion? Everything.

Religion utilizes and piggybacks onto everyday social-thought processes, adaptive psychological mechanisms that evolved to help us negotiate our relationships with other people, to detect agency and intent, and to generate a sense of safety. These mechanisms were forged in the not-so-distant world of our African homeland. They are why we survived.

While not an adaptation in its own right, religious belief is a by-product of those psychological mechanisms that allowed us to imagine other people and other social worlds, abilities crucial to human survival. Because religion only slightly alters those adaptations, it can be equally powerful.

Let's look at the workings of adaptive by-products another way: do you like fast food—say, a big, juicy burger with cheese, a large side of crisp, salted fries, and an icy cola or shake? Most people like some kind of fast food, at times even crave it. If fast food doesn't tempt you, maybe you occasionally crave a succulent prime rib. Or ice cream. You may avoid them for dietary or health reasons, but odds are that you at least occasionally break down and buy such meals, even against your better judgment.

Why does this matter? If you understand the psychology of craving fast food, a savory slice of prime rib, or a decadent chocolate sundae, you can fully comprehend the psychology of religion.

We evolved in harsh, dangerous environments. We evolved cravings for foods that were rare and crucial to our physical well-being. Nobody craves Brussels sprouts. Certain types of greens and tubers were an available source of food in the ancient world. But we all crave fat, and we all crave sweets.

The original fat was game meat, an invaluable source of concentrated protein and calories. The original sweets were ripe fruit, important sources of calories, nutrients, and vitamin C. Plentiful food was nonexistent. Starvation was always right around the corner.

Craving is an adaptation. It solves the problem of securing crucial but rare life-sustaining foods. When our ancestors experienced cravings, they sought those foods out, and because of that survived and reproduced better than those who did not inherit this particular adaptation, and thus did not crave the foods they needed.

And once they found those foods, whenever they could, our ancestors ate more than they needed at that moment. In the world in which we evolved, they couldn't expect to find that food again tomorrow. That eat-more-than-you-need appetite and adaptation helped solve the problem of unpredictable food availability.

But today, in most areas of the developed world, food is plentiful and human culture has created new ways of responding to these cravings. Now we have fast food, high in unhealthy fat that plugs our arteries and expands our waistlines, a far cry from the lean game meat our ancestors sought out. Instead of ripe fruits we have sodas and candy bars.

Even knowing the harm eating fat, salt, and sugar can do to us, we still crave them, and unless disciplined, we will choose them over lean meat and ripe fruit. Why?

Because they pack supernormal stimuli. Our brains react to this relatively recent rise of excessive calories on demand as if it's a good thing, as though we still need to behave as our ancestors did. Our brains reward us. When we eat our favorite food, the pleasure centers in our brain explode with delight. What we experience is not just slight satisfaction, but an intense pleasure released by brain chemicals. Those centers in our brain, mediated by the neurotransmitter dopamine, are called "do-it-again" centers. Not only do they give us a wave of pleasure, they motivate us to repeat the action that brought us such satisfaction.

The pleasure sensation also is an adaptation. It originally helped solve the problem of searching for and securing crucial foods by reinforcing their consumption, rewarding the find, and causing the craving that ensured survival to continue.

So, our illogical craving for these new cultural creations arises from adaptations that helped ensure survival—the cravings that caused our ancestors to seek out fats or sweets, which helped them survive. But these modern foods, packed with more fat and sugar than anything our ancestors ever found or killed, satisfy the cravings with far more intense emotional reward and consequent stimuli than the original game meat or ripe fruit ever provided.

This is why it is not a joke to say that if you understand the psychology of fast food, you understand the psychology of religion. With the design of fast food, we have unconsciously hijacked ancient adaptations to crave and subsequently secure the essential fats and sweets that kept our ancestors alive and fit to reproduce.

We didn't evolve to crave fast food, but our brains still accept it as adaptive. These fast-food cravings are a by-product. And now they become dangerous, because, uncontrolled, they can lead to health problems our ancestors likely never faced.

Which brings us to religion—or, more specifically, the adaptations from which belief stems.

Is what we crave always good for us?

3

Our Daily Bread
Craving a Caretaker

> *We must, however, acknowledge, as it seems to me, that man with all his noble qualities. . . still bears in his bodily frame the indelible stamp of his lowly origin.*
>
> —Charles Darwin

Running in the background of our minds is a myriad of survival-based mental capacities waiting to be deployed. These help us navigate the world, especially the social world. We barely notice them, and even when we do, we take them for granted, but they are fascinating and were indispensible for our survival as we evolved, and still are. These adaptations are the building blocks of religious beliefs.

The Attachment System
As the song says, we all need someone to lean on.

The *attachment system* is one of our most powerful adaptations. Our species could not have survived, much less evolved, without it. When most of us are distressed, we seek out or turn to a caretaker. This driving need begins the day we leave the womb—and from a strictly neurochemical point of view, possibly sooner.

First described by British psychiatrist John Bowlby in the 1940s, and later elaborated on and demonstrated by Canadian-American psychologist Mary Ainsworth in a series of controlled experiments with mother and child, the attachment system is the basis of the child-parent bond. It is a legacy of our mammalian heritage that goes back tens of millions of years or more.

Neuroscientists now believe that attachment is such a primal need that networks of neurons in the brain are dedicated to it, and the process of forming lasting bonds is powered in part by oxytocin, a neuropeptide that we'll discuss more a bit later.

When we are young and helpless, attachment solves the problem of finding and latching onto our principle source of protection and survival. When we are older, the attachment system is used in romantic love. After the glow of romance fades in any sustained partnership, the attachment system remains. It uses the original parent-child bond mechanism to cement the ties between adults.

Attachment also affects other adult relationships. Close friendships take advantage of it; this is why you turn to certain friends and not others when times are tough. As we evolved and formed small groups, attachment to mates and other adults aided our survival as individuals and as a species.

One haunting example of the attachment system in our ancestors comes from paleoanthropologists Alan Walker and Pat Shipman's description of a *Homo erectus* woman whose fossilized remains were discovered in Africa. The fossils clearly showed that she had died of vitamin A poisoning, probably from eating an animal liver. It's likely that after the poisoning, she had lived for weeks, or months, with hemorrhaging into the joints and terrible pain.

The woman would not have survived on the savannahs more than a million years ago without a caretaker. Someone must have brought her food and water, and protected her from predators throughout the African nights.

Today, we see the attachment system every day in our lives and in our own relationships with friends, lovers, spouses, and children. In fact, the attachment system as such is commonly if not always consciously accepted. Not only are people attached to family, they are also attached to their pets, their lovers, their close friends. Even Charlie Brown's friend Linus is attached to his blanket, as any young child might be attached to a favorite stuffed animal. All make us feel secure and safe.

And, of course, religious people are attached to their gods. It is no leap of faith to see how the attachment system works not just in corporeal dealings but also in the human propensity to desire attachment to a religious structure, as well as to an unchanging, loving, and eternal being.

Think of a two-year-old child reaching out to be picked up and cuddled. He extends his hands above his head and beseeches you. Think now of the Pentecostal worshipper who speaks in tongues. He stretches out his hands above his head, beseeching god in the same "pick-me-up-and-hold-me" gesture. We may lose human attachment figures through death, through misunderstandings, through distance, but a god is always there for us.

We see this often in practical psychiatry. A young woman patient who had been physically, emotionally, and verbally abused by her father sought in her Christian religion his opposite: a considerate father who would love her and accept her love. She would ask for guidance from god for life decisions, talk to him as a young adult would to a supportive and knowledgeable parent, and worry about his reaction as a young woman would fret about a father's reaction.

The fact is that we never lose the longing for a caretaker.

Who will protect you and your loved ones from starvation, illness, disaster, death, and the other misfortunes of life? Your parents? When you were little, before you even knew the concept of deity, they were the definition of gods, able to do anything. Today, if they are still alive, you know them as the ordinary human beings they are, with no more power than you have to protect, to soothe wounds, and to stem the tides of fortune and fate that rush us headlong through life. They may even now depend on you.

An omniscient and omnipotent sky parent might, if beseeched often and with great intensity, not only protect us and our loved ones, but also help us find community in like-minded people, shield us from the fear of death, assure our salvation, and provide an afterlife that more than compensates for all of our human suffering. This is religion's promise. Our parents cannot take care of us forever, but Yahweh can. There are no atheists in foxholes.

Religions give us supernormal "parents," magnificent attachment figures the likes of which we never experience in everyday life, and never can. When we are distressed, we turn to a god that hears our prayers, grants our wishes, protects our loved ones, and reassures us of reward no matter how adverse our troubles.

Like those now counterproductive fast-food cravings, religious ideas arise from adaptations, but today's religions provide supernormal stimuli and excessively intense rewards that can trigger a desperate search for more. Like the fast-food craving, religious ideas arise from adaptations that kept our ancestors alive—but that doesn't mean those cravings are good for us.

Which do you prefer, tofu or steak? Broccoli or a hot fudge sundae? Which gives you a greater rush of pleasure?

Attachment and Rejection

This need for attachment contributes both to the ease of accepting religion and to the difficulty in rejecting it. Quite simply, we want to believe in something loving and eternal.

We can see it in Charles Darwin's own life. When he went on his famous voyage of the *Beagle*, from 1831 to 1836, he was a creationist. When he returned, he gave his Galapagos bird specimens to ornithologist John Gould. Darwin had already considered the possibility that species were not immutable, not fixed in time—not, to be specific, the unchanging creation of a god. When Gould told him the Galapagos birds were species of finch unknown to nature and not previously described, it became clear to him that species changed according to environment and over time.

In the summer of 1837, Darwin opened his famous notebooks and drew out a tree of life, illustrating the idea that species evolved. And he noted that "man in his arrogance thinks himself a great work, worthy of the interposition of a great deity. More humble, and I believe true, to consider him created from animals."

Darwin did not yet understand the mechanism by which this change in species over time occurred. In September of 1838, he read T. R. Malthus's "Essay on the Principles of Population," which postulated that animals produced far more young than could survive. He came to believe there was a struggle for existence, and those who had what it took to survive and reproduce were those who continued into the future. He had figured it out.

But even Darwin had a hard time rejecting religion. He was, at the time, engaged to his religious first cousin, Emma Wedgewood. Somewhere in the fall of 1838 he must have told her about his ideas. She wrote, in a letter to him that survives, "My reason tells me that honest and conscientious doubts cannot be a sin, but I feel it would be a painful void between us." They married in January of 1839.

He certainly had his idea of natural selection worked out by then, but it remained unpublished for twenty years, likely at least in part because of the distress he knew publication would cause his wife. But by the 1850s, the difference between them could be seen on Sunday mornings. He would walk with Emma and the children to church. She and the children would go into the church, and Darwin would continue to walk. His beloved daughter Annie had died from tuberculosis; with her died Darwin's religious belief.

A year before he died in 1881, as he was finishing his autobiography, Darwin reread a letter from Emma written in February of 1839, in which she wrote: "May not the habits in scientific pursuits of believing nothing until it is proved, influence your mind too much in other things which cannot be proved."

A devout Christian, Emma likely was distressed by his ideas, and certainly by his lack of faith. At the bottom of that letter he inscribed, "When I am dead, know that many times I have kissed and cryed over this. C. D."

Not only is the attachment system a crucial part of religious faith, it is probably one of the adaptations that makes departure from it difficult. Carl Giberson, in his book *Saving Darwin: How to Be a Christian and Believe in Evolution*, wrote: "I have a compelling reason to believe in God. My parents are deeply committed Christians and would be devastated, were I to reject my faith. My wife and children believe in God . . . abandoning belief in God would be disruptive, sending my life completely off the rails."

But our loved ones don't need to tell us outright that departure from what had been a shared belief, or the unwillingness to share their beliefs, will make them unhappy. We know this intuitively, because other uniquely human adaptations—now parts of the basic design of our brain—allow us to infer their reactions to our decisions, even if they say nothing. It begins with our ability to mentally separate their minds from their bodies, which in turn circles back to our ability not only to believe in what we cannot see but also to interact with the invisible. We are born with the ability to read what others' may be thinking even when they are not there to tell us. In a way, all of those to whom we are attached sometimes become imaginary friends.

4

All That Is Seen and Unseen
Conceiving Souls

The highest possible stage in moral culture is when we recognize that we ought to control our thoughts.

—Charles Darwin

The Mind-Body Split

Because we need to work with other people to survive, our brains evolved the ability to make assumptions about others, to create conjecture to help us coexist in social settings. We are born accepting that others are like us, intentional agents with minds like ours, even though we are unable to literally see their minds.

One aspect of this is called the *mind-body split* or *dualism*, the view that the mind and body function separately, without interchange. We cannot conceive of souls unless we see mind as separate from body. And we do, because our brains are wired that way.

The medial frontal area of our brains, just behind the space between the eyes, contains the circuits for introspection, awareness of our own nonphysical attributes, our emotional states and traits, and our own wishes and desires. It is also the part of our brain with which we reflect on the abstract: other people's minds, their intentions, beliefs, desires, and feelings—*their* nonphysical attributes.

This ability is not learned; it is innate, hardwired. The brain represents mind and body in separate neural circuits. This allows us to separate minds from bodies, to experience and believe that they are entirely different categories

The lateral part of the brain is where we recognize concrete, visible things such as our own faces and bodies and the movements of others in relation to them. It is also where we note out-of-the-ordinary aspects of our situations, such as something moving that should not.

Religious ideas are influential and endure because they fit neatly with this structure, this mind-body split.

Like many of the concepts so crucial to religion, the split between animate and inanimate can be seen in infants and children. A five-month-old who sees a box move on its own will startle. But a moving *person* is a normal part of everyday life and causes not a ruffle from that same child. It is natural in the child's brain to think of animate intentional agents, but an inanimate physical property—the box—should not move like an intentional agent—the person.

In a revealing experiment with children, Jesse Bering, a psychologist at Queens University in Ireland, created a puppet show. In the show, a puppet alligator swallows a puppet mouse. Bering then asked the children various questions about the mouse. Does the mouse still eat? Does the mouse miss its mother? The children knew the mouse could no longer eat, but they thought it missed its mother. These young children attributed to a dead mouse a mental state that they were unable to conceive no longer exists.

This concept often shows up in debates about abortion rights as some variant of the question, "How would you feel if *you* had been aborted?"

Bering's simple but brilliant experiment shows that even children demonstrate the mind-body split; this means that belief in the supernatural is not something learned from our culture as we grow from infants into toddlers and more cognizant children. It is original equipment, requiring no social prompting.

Children also demonstrate another aspect of this foundation of religious belief. Almost half of all four-year-olds have imaginary friends. It turns out that those who do generally grow up to be more socially competent. In many ways, a god is our imaginary friend.

Whatever version of the supernatural our culture imparts to us, it lands on a mind already biased to accept that human mental life and capacities float free of a living or dead body. The supernatural beliefs of religion merely pirate the way our brain is designed to think about other people, their minds, and their intentions. The mind and all that fills it remains separate from the body.

Understanding the attachment system and the mind-body split is just the beginning of understanding the ways in which the mind can be tricked into belief.

5

Because the Bible Tells Me So
Believing in the Invisible

> *Beautiful as is the morality of the New Testament, it can hardly be denied that its perfection depends in part on the interpretation which we now put on metaphors and allegories.*
>
> —Charles Darwin

Decoupled Cognition

Imagine that the only way you could think about what might be going on in another person's mind was for that person to be sitting in front of you. Human relationships as we know them would be impossible, and the same was also true for our ancestors. We need to evaluate the likely thoughts and feelings of others, even when those others are nowhere to be seen.

For this reason, human beings are uniquely adapted to accept the presence of disembodied entities and to assume they will behave in certain ways. Most of us do it every day.

Have you ever thought of a perfect response to a conversational challenge when it was too late to use it, and mentally replayed how the conversation could have gone? Lain awake at night agonizing about fixing a social or career misstep? Mentally rehearsed a marriage proposal, or a request for a raise?

We humans have the remarkable ability to create and implement a complex interaction with an unseen other—boss, spouse, friend—in our minds, regardless of time or place, in the past or in the future. You had an argument. You were wrong. You want to apologize but you need to plan how. You mentally rehearse it, envisioning how the other person will respond. And all of this occurs while you go about your daily life.

This is called *decoupled cognition*, and it is key to religious belief.

We can decouple our cognition from time, place, and circumstance. This ability arises in childhood and is seen vividly in play. A child might say a bottle cap is a flying saucer. The child knows what it really is but can choose to ignore the reality and think of it as a flying saucer, with the attributes imagined and related to as such. The child is decoupling his or her cognition.

Theater and filmgoers use such "suspension of disbelief" all the time. They know that what is happening on the stage or screen is not real. Yet, when watching, they choose to believe that the people on the stage or screen really exist, that they live in another place and time, that the car really was blown to smithereens, that a character came back to life.

As adults, this mechanism is crucial to memory and planning. We can go back and forth in time, place, and circumstance as we think how to manage the relationships in our lives. We remember the meeting with the boss. We plan a conversation for the future. All this interaction is with others who are not there at the moment.

Interacting in our minds with unseen others is natural. Many people mentally converse with recently departed loved ones. A natural extension of this—a leap of faith, if you will— can become ancestor worship and belief in gods. Our mind's ability to create a complex relationship with unseen others simply expands.

Theory-of-Mind Mechanisms

Closely related to decoupled cognition is an amazing mental capacity, systems in our brain called *theory-of-mind mechanisms*, an understated name for an amazing gift. Before we can imagine how someone might react, we have to somehow understand what and how that person probably thinks. And, for the most part, we are able to do that. We have an innate ability to "read" what another person may think, believe, desire, or intend, in remarkable detail and with remarkable accuracy, and make assumptions based on that.

Think of people you know well. You can probably fairly accurately imagine what issues they might be considering at this very moment. You can make an educated guess as to what they think of you. This ability likely helped our ancestors determine who was friend and who was not, interact socially, and plan accordingly for survival.

This ability for joint attention may be the key to human uniqueness. Alone among the apes, we engage in complex cooperation with others, not only reading others' minds but also reading others reading our minds. We take it for granted because it seems so simple. But it is not.

For example, you and I plan to meet at a theater for the 9 p.m. movie. We have constructed a plan to cooperate in a joint venture. Each knows of the other's commitment to the task. But you know I can be late. So you told me to be there on time, and I know you are frustrated with my tendency to be late. And you know I know of your displeasure with my tardiness. When I arrive in plenty of time for the movie, you smile. I know you are pleased at my punctuality, and you know I see and understand your pleasure. Not a single word need be said.

It is just one small step to imagining an amorphous humanlike mind with ideas, feelings, and intentions about you and your fellow man. We can imagine this humanlike mind and engage in a joint venture. We'll build a cathedral with and for him. He'll be pleased. We'll know he's pleased if good fortune comes our way.

Intensionality

A closely related phenomenon is intensionality, spelled with an "s." This is another extraordinary, taken-for-granted mental capacity. It goes like this:

First Order	"I think."
Second Order	"I think you think."
Third Order	"I think you think that I think."
Fourth Order	"I think you think that I think that you think."

Let's try it this way:

First Order	"I hope."
Second Order	"I hope you like this book."
Third Order	"I know you are aware that I hope you like this book."
Fourth Order	"You can be certain that I know that you are aware that I hope you like this book."

These can, of course, be colored by circumstance. Imagine a social situation. A woman is talking to a man she thinks is boring. But the man thinks the woman considers him very attractive. In a corner of the room, watching, is the woman's husband, who suspects that his wife is flirting with the other man, because he knows she is angry with him and believes she is retaliating—which, in fact, she may be doing, knowing that it will annoy her husband.

This kind of awareness of what other people think, and what other people think about what we might think, is something that is utterly indispensable for social relationships.

Religions easily utilize intensionality.

First Order	"I believe."
Second Order	"I believe that God wants."
Third Order	"I believe that God wants us to act with righteous intent."
Fourth Order	"I want you to believe that God wants us to act with righteous intent."
Fifth Order	"I want you to know that we both believe that God wants us to act with righteous intent."

Psychologist Robin Dunbar notes that third-order intensionality is "personal religion." But, for you to be convinced, there must be fourth-order intensionality—someone else adds to your mind state, asking you to believe. That produces "social religion."

Even if you accept the truth of social religion, it commits you to nothing. If you add the fifth order, you accept the claim, become a believer, and have created "communal religion." Together people can invoke obligations and demand that others behave in prescribed ways.

You see this capacity for shared intensionality develop in infants long before they can speak. Take a young child, sit him on the floor, and roll or bounce a ball back and forth with him. He easily joins in the game. Then bounce the ball so that it lands out of either of your reach. The child will retrieve the ball, put it in your hand, and gesture to resume the game. He knows you know the game and that you know that he wants to play again.

This shared intensionality on joint action may even be the basis of language. If you and I are English speakers, we each know the other knows that the arbitrary term "book" signals what this is. If we are French, then we each know, and know the other knows, that the arbitrary convention is "*livre.*"

Making relatively accurate assumptions about others can play a part even when we encounter people we don't know, or don't know well. We evolved separate, dedicated adaptations to assess eye gaze, perhaps one of the reasons eyes are called "windows to the soul." We can pick up much information about others from their eyes, which may have allowed our ancestors to determine hostility in others within or outside of their tribes, or to know friend from enemy in chance encounters. If you've ever encountered the steady gaze of a baby who doesn't know you, you have seen this in action.

This mental ability has been demonstrated by Psychologist Simon Baron-Cohen of Cambridge University, who showed in startling detail our mental ability to read, with a fair degree of accuracy, several hundred discrete emotional states in other people simply from looking at their eyes. In short, we can make complex judgments about a person we don't know and a mind/brain we can never directly see.

Transference

Calling a god our father taps not only into our wiring for attachment but also into an adaptation called *transference,* which is particularly useful in understanding certain aspects of religion.

All of us unconsciously base life relationships on earlier relationships. Just as we learn to walk and talk early in life, we learn strategies for dealing with others. These early relationship strategies form enduring personality characteristics, for better or for worse becoming the grammar we use to conduct later relationships.

For example, as adults, we relate to authority figures in the same ways we did in our formative years. We assume these new authorities will respond to us as such people did in our past, and we base our attitude toward present figures on those earlier experiences. If those earliest experiences were harsh, we make the assumption that current authorities will treat us badly. We adjust our relationship to them accordingly, even when that is not the case and the present authority is actually kindly disposed toward us.

But why did the capacity for transference evolve in the human mind? What problems does it solve? What adaptive function does it serve?

We use the shorthand of transference to assign to others feelings and attitudes we originally associated with important figures in our early lives. In the best of circumstances, basing present relationships on past relationships—real, imagined, or wished for—is an efficient way of anticipating outcomes. Imagine what it would be like if we had to relearn how to relate to people with each new social relationship.

Every day, psychotherapists see the many ways that disturbed early relationships distort present relationships. When that transference is repeated in psychoanalytic therapy, the details of the transference itself become the arena for treatment.

But what does this have to do with religion? Think of all the potential transferences mobilized by religious belief. Christians look to God the Father, Mary the Mother, and so on. Then think of how those beliefs can combine with personal transference: human parents, siblings, and significant others. Psychotherapeutic treatment of religious individuals often unmasks early relationships that transfer and contribute to the patient's religious beliefs.

6

And Deliver Us from Evil
Anthropomorphizing God(s)

The very essence of instinct is that it's followed independently of reason.

—Charles Darwin

Another uniquely human attribute that favors religion is our predisposition to ascribe humanlike power or influence (agency) to nearly everything we encounter.

Why is it you mistake a shadow for a burglar but never a burglar for a shadow? If you hear a door slam, why do you wonder who did it before you consider the wind as the culprit? Why might a child who sees blowing tree limbs through a window fear that it's the boogeyman come to get him? For that matter, where did the nearly universal childhood concept of a "boogeyman" or monsters under the bed come from? Some psychologists think the monster under the bed may be a legacy of our early life as australopithecines. We spent the night in trees with predators lurking below and retain that vigilance to dangers below.

Humans are strongly biased to interpret unclear evidence as being caused consciously by an agent, almost always a humanlike agent. This cognitive ability to attribute agency to abstract sights or sounds may have helped our distant ancestors survive, allowing them to detect and evade enemies. It kept them alert, attentive toward possible danger. Better to jump at shadows than risk something or someone jumping at you.

Hyperactive Agency Detection Device

This ability is always triggered quickly (hyperactive) and easily deployed (hypersensitive). It has been called *hyperactive agency detection device*. This device contributes to religious beliefs because it allows and even favors inference of unseen agents, almost always human or humanlike agents. Once the mind makes such a connection, it is an easy leap to belief in a ghost or spirit, even an all-powerful one.

This ability was adaptive, so therefore it is natural for us to assume the presence of unseen beings and to believe that such beings can influence our lives. It is equally natural to assume that such a being, if asked, can alter or affect what happens to us. Asking easily becomes praying.

With the assistance of evolved face detectors and other cognitive capacities sensitive to human forms, the human mind can see humanlike figures almost anywhere—the Man in the Moon, the cantankerous apple trees in Oz, Jesus on a potato chip, a smiley face in punctuation marks :-).

People even see the "Eye of God" in a color-enhanced composite photo of the Helix nebula partly taken from NASA's Hubble telescope, the image on the cover of this book.

Another manifestation may occur when we ascribe agency to known nonagents, such as a storm cloud or the wind. You might say "the sky looks angry today," or "this wind is brutal." The ancient Greeks took it a step further: Zeus threw lightning bolts, Poseidon caused storms at sea, and shipwrecks were caused by seductive and destructive Sirens.

Now, you may ask, wait a second, how do decoupled cognition and hyperactive agency lead to supernatural beliefs? How do we move beyond mental conversations with ancestors and jumping at shadows to supernatural belief?

We already attribute agency to very ordinary things and are automatically willing to accept the invisible and even to fear them or it.

As social beings with these adaptations, we are now set up for belief in a divine attachment figure. We can attribute agency to it, transfer some of our early-life emotions to it, and as a result can believe that such a being desires to interact with us. But this being remains invisible and largely imaginary, with clear missing pieces. How does it turn into a god?

Inferential Reasoning and Minimally Counterintuitive Worlds

We fill in blanks. That is inferential reasoning. Filling in the blanks without even thinking about it, operating with certain basic assumptions unstated, is the foundation of *minimally counterintuitive worlds*.

Look at the below image. There are no lines in the picture, but you see a square. You have inferred the square from the available evidence, filled in the blanks, so to speak. If you text message, you use and see inferential reasoning every day.

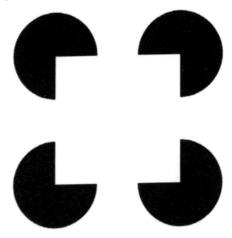

Filling in the blanks, combined with other adaptations, helps us create a complete picture from an almost-complete one. If a small element or two is a little different, but not entirely off base, we can still see and accept the picture. It is still minimally counterintuitive. This is the basis for minimally counterintuitive worlds, which are an optimal compromise between the interesting and the expected. One quirk of human minds is that these minimally counterintuitive worlds are attention arresting and memorable.

If you are told that the big oak tree in the park near your home will do your taxes, wash your laundry, fix your car, and tell you what your future stock portfolio will be, you will not even experiment with belief. Why? There are simply too many violations of "treeness."

However, if you're told that the tree will hear your prayer during a full moon, you may be vulnerable to believing. It certainly will be an easily remembered description. Why? Because it's only a hair's breadth from reality. Although a few human mental capacities, such as the ability to listen and comprehend human speech and to act in response, have been attributed to the tree, it is still a tree. Its primary attribute remains a tree, rooted in the park, subject to all that we understand about and expect of a tree. Yet we find the slight addition of magic intriguing.

Consider the fairy tales you heard as a child: a beautiful queen disguises herself as a wicked witch but easily transforms back; a wicked witch has a cottage made of candy to lure children; a stepdaughter servant girl can become beautiful and marry the handsome prince.

It is our ability to construct and connect to these minimally counterintuitive worlds that lies at the heart of our propensity to generate and accept religious ideas and suspend disbelief. Just as fairy tales are close enough to reality for children to believe, the core architecture of all religions involves a slight twist in some physical, biological, or psychological property of a basic object that otherwise remains the same, and comfortably familiar.

With minimally counterintuitive worlds, the supernatural always remains connected to the ordinary and everyday worlds. This aspect not only makes them memorable, but more important, also allows them to relieve core existential human problems that are rationally intractable, such as death.

Ancient Egyptians worshipped the cat goddess Bastet. It was not much of a stretch to go from sleek creatures snoozing in sunbeams by day and efficiently purging granaries of rodents and reptiles by night to a goddess that traveled across the skies with the sun-god Ra, protected humans from contagious diseases and evil spirits, and fought Ra's arch-enemy, the serpent Apap. At its core, Bastet is still a cat keeping disease-carrying rodents and poisonous reptiles at bay.

The twist might be more counterintuitive, but the rest is seated in reality. The Virgin Mary conceived Jesus while still a virgin, but everything else about young womanness and motherhood remained intact.

The Judeo-Christian god is physically everywhere. He knows my thoughts. He knows if I have been naughty or nice in my mind. But everything else about god remains simply human. Otherwise he is just a guy, and everything you know about men remains intact. God can be surly, impatient, vengeful, and in most ways a regular fellow.

We fill in the blanks, and we fail to even notice it, much less think about it.

Religions always assign simple, mundane human capacities to gods. Christians believe that Jesus was a man and god. All normal human attributes are there, and we relate to the god accordingly along those dimensions. We are never aware of this unless we actually think about it and catch such contradictions as the need to pray to a mind reader. Gods are assumed to perceive, feel, and act like ordinary folk, and behave like the best and worst of us. These basic operating assumptions about gods are always there, embedded like bricks in the wall of any foundation.

Why would people have to pray? If our god reads and knows our thoughts, why would we need to talk to him? The Bible answers that question: God only hears us if we ask him to. And we are back to rationalizing religion.

Are we deceiving ourselves?

Self-Deception

If we deceive ourselves, we can easily deceive others. Ambitious politicians may genuinely believe that they are running for office to promote a particular cause. In fact, they could be hiding their own ambitions and hunger for power and status even from themselves.

Arthur Miller's powerful 1947 play *All My Sons*, which was based on a true story, illustrates the power of self-deception. In the play, a man who runs a war factory knowingly ships out faulty parts, causing the death of twenty-one pilots. For more than three years, he fools others and himself, blaming his jailed partner. When the truth comes out, the man claims he acted for his family, to keep the factory running, and fully believes it. The play is largely about how his self-deception is slowly unraveled, and he is forced to face the truth.

This human ability for self-deception is crucial to religious belief. If many believers could see their own minds more clearly, they would see that self-deception plays a role in their acceptance of faith.

Maybe there are *only* atheists in foxholes. If the faithful truly and fully believe in a protective deity, why would they dive into a foxhole to protect themselves from the bullets whizzing by? A part of their brains knows damn well that if they do not protect themselves, the bullets will hardly discriminate between those who claim faith and those who reject it. They may say and think they believe, but their instinctive actions expose the lie.

Why do the faithful buy health insurance? House insurance? Most people live their lives as if there is no god. We stop at red lights, we put our children in car seats, and we act responsibly to protect our safety and the safety of those we love. Consider the bumper sticker that reads, "Caution: In Case of Rapture This Car Will Be Driverless!" Even there, the driver is warning other drivers. If a person is religious, he is an atheist in relation to others' gods and the gods of history. He also will almost invariably live as an atheist in relation to his own worshipped deity.

We expect others to live as atheists too. We want them to stop at red lights and not assume we drive under divine protection. We in the West have become so used to religious people *not* really, truly, and fully believing what they say they believe that we are startled when, as on 9/11, we encounter people who really do believe their religion and put their beliefs into murderous practice.

Overreading Determination

Just like the husband who thought his bored wife was flirting, we have minds wildly biased to *overread determination*, especially human determination or purpose. Of course, we are barely aware of it. It is there when we say, "It rained today because I didn't bring my umbrella." Even atheists may claim an event happened in his or her life "for a purpose."

The bias to read purpose and design when it does not exist is most obvious in children. If you ask a child what lakes are for, she might say for fish to swim in. What are birds for? To sing. What are rocks for? For animals to scratch themselves. Millions of parents probably have nearly hit the breaking point when their three-year-old asks, for the billionth time, "Why?"

Children have been described as "intuitive theists." Children show what is called *promiscuous teleology*, a basic preference to understand the world in terms of purpose. This contributes to what we now know about children's belief. Children will spontaneously adopt the concept of God and a created world with no adult intervention. At heart we are all born creationists. Disbelief requires effort.

Even adults are far from paragons of rationality. We too need to see purpose. In fact, the need to see purpose is inherent in the definition of religion. For example, Dictionary.com defines religion first as "a set of beliefs concerning the cause, nature, and purpose of the universe, especially when considered as the creation of a superhuman agency or agencies, usually involving devotional and ritual observances."

Bible literalists believe that animals exist for the sole purpose of serving humanity. That nonhuman animals have played a role of their own in the evolution of our species and the ecosystem of our planet isn't something literalists consider.

Our problem with purpose is most manifest in our resistance to and difficulty understanding natural selection. Because we expect that "everything happens for a reason," it is hard for us to wrap our minds around how life evolved. It's hard for us to accept the gradual and random mutation of genes and the nonrandom survival of the bodies that contain them. Our bias to overread purpose and our baseline inability to comprehend the blind, purposeless mechanics of life's evolution can make religious belief the path of least resistance.

We have an innate need for order in our lives, and religion fills it.

7

Thy Will Be Done
Submitting to the Law of God(s)

Such social qualities, the paramount importance of which to the lower animals is disputed by no one, were no doubt acquired by the progenitors of man in a similar manner, namely, through natural selection, aided by inherited habit.

—Charles Darwin

Deference to Authority

We are far more *deferential to authority* than any of us would like to admit. This was revealed in a set of famous experiments conducted by Stanley Milgram, a psychologist at Yale University, beginning in 1961. Milgram demonstrated that about two-thirds of normal individuals will continue to administer an electric shock to a helpless "learner," against their own wishes, if commanded to do so by an authority. If you are unfamiliar with the Milgram experiments, take a few moments and research them on the Web. You will be shocked by both the original experiments and those that have replicated Milgram's findings.

The emotions of awe and respect are part of our makeup, designed to motivate our behaviors toward those in authority and higher on the social hierarchy. Those feelings are easy targets for religions. Honor thy father and thy mother. Praise and submit to whatever god(s) rules your particular faith.

Morality

The second part of the first definition of religion given by Dictionary.com is ". . . and often containing a moral code governing the conduct of human affairs." There are those who say that without religion man would be amoral and lawless. They are, quite simply, wrong.

We are born moral animals. We don't need religion to keep us from being immoral monsters, as some faiths would have us believe. If our ancestors had no sense of right and wrong, however their groups interpreted the terms, they could not long have survived in social groups.

In addition to the presence of mirror neurons, which we will discuss in chapter 9, other evidence refutes the concept that morality is learned behavior only, without inborn aspects.

Human arrogance leads us to think we alone are moral beings. Other animals demonstrate empathy, compassion, grief, comfort, assistance, forgiveness, trust, reciprocity, and a sense of justice, revenge, spite, and much more. When acknowledged, those traits have been downplayed as "building blocks" of human morality. Instead, they should be seen as composing the evolved moral systems needed for a particular social species' behavior.

The evolution of *moral behaviors* goes hand in hand with the evolution of sociality. Social complexity builds moral complexity. And we are one very social species.

In his groundbreaking research, Yale psychology professor Paul Bloom and his team found that infants as young as three months old have some innate sense of right and wrong, good and bad, even fair and unfair.

When shown a puppet climbing a mountain, either helped or hindered by a second puppet, the babies oriented toward the helpful puppet and away from the second one. They were able to make an evaluative social judgment, in a sense a moral response. He notes that "it is often beneficial for humans to work together . . . which means it would have been adaptive to evaluate the niceness and nastiness of other individuals. All this is reason to consider the innateness of at least basic moral concepts."

The example we gave you in chapter 5, about a young child playing a game with a ball on the floor, comes from the work of Michael Tomasello, the developmental psychologist who codirects the Max Planck Institute for Evolutionary Anthropology in Leipzig, Germany. He and his colleagues have produced a wealth of research that demonstrates very young children's innate capacities. He argues we are born altruists who then have to learn strategic self-interest.

Tomasello's group shows children's ability to assess a situation and engage in complex helping behaviors, replete with a clear sense of fairness. Felix Warneken's video of toddlers stumbling away from their mothers to help open a cabinet for a tall man brings home the point with sheer delight.

Our moral systems are like our innate grammar; we all have the ability to learn a language, and we learn the language of our culture. All of us have moral systems, and we learn the moral values of our culture. We internalize them, and those values color our intuitive, automatic, and emotional moral responses. We know the difference between right and wrong even without religion.

Our morality seems to be a dual system that involves both unconscious and automatic process, as well as an after-the-fact conscious process that has been localized to specific areas of the brain.

It appears that our emotional moral processes reside in the orbitofrontal cortex, at the bottom midsection of our brains. Those areas constantly monitor our environment, particularly our social environment, and our place in it. When there are alterations in that environment, we react automatically. If the alteration is positive, we approach; if it is negative, we avoid. There is an instant, emotional evaluative process.

Several areas trigger our moral responses. Harm and unfairness are the first; if we see violations in those domains, we respond. All people respond to certain cues automatically, though learned cultural differences determine the intensity and shadings of our responses.

Although we are all much more deferential to authority than any of us would suspect, as the Milgram experiments proved, we do have moral emotions that help us negotiate our relationships with authority, allowing us to somehow define in-groups to which we are loyal. We deem their actions good, and we defend them. We also identify out-groups of which we remain wary, determining that they are suspect and not to be trusted until they demonstrate otherwise. Religions have served as a ready-made mechanism to define death-deserving out-groups.

Purity seems another dimension of our automatic moral emotions. Perhaps it arose from our disgust feelings at putrid meat, which protected us from disease, but that disgust reaction can carry over into social relationships. Disgust has become a powerful moralizing emotion, brought in to enhance criticism and condemnation. It is often directed toward those labeled as the out-group. Feelings of purity inform our sense of people, places, or items tagged as sacred, and our discomfort when rituals or the sacred are violated or "contaminated."

Our conscious moral feelings are rationalization processes that allow us to justify our automatic emotional responses. To understand this, compare moral responses to aesthetic judgments. When you see a painting you like, you just like it. It moves you somehow. When asked why, you come up with reasons, but they are essentially rationalizations that may or may not at all relate to whatever that positive gut reaction was.

We have similar automatic moral reactions, and we can then, like a good lawyer, build a conscious case to justify them. That "lawyer" part of our brain, which has been localized to the cerebral cortex, the brain's outer layer, will give the reasons for any moral reaction and will build our case. Sometimes that part of our brain can override our emotional response, and we might find someone we "instinctively" detest innocent.

Since so much of our moral emotional processes are unconscious, religion can make our lives easier by assigning for us conscious reasons to feelings that arise seemingly out of nowhere and with no conscious processing.

It is quite possible to be nonreligious but highly moral. But if you followed the exact wording of the Bible, you could sell your uppity daughter into slavery (Exodus 21:7). Other religious works have equally odd provisions. Ancient scriptures seem full of moral advice that sounds anything but moral to the modern listener. The less you abide by scripture, and the more you use your basic moral intuitions, the more moral you are likely to be.

Genuine morality is doing what is right regardless of what we may be told; religious morality is doing what we are told. Religion's power gives us strong reasons to do what we're told. Religion allows us to be part of an in-group that will reap eternal reward or it can prevent us from burning in hell for eternity.

People who have abandoned religion will also tell you that having religious belief is much easier than not having it, requiring, as it does, so much less mental effort than making one's own decisions.

Kin Psychology

Humans evolved and are born with elegant mind mechanisms to recognize and relate to *kin*, to favor relatives over strangers. It is captured in the old saying, "Me against my brother, my brother and I against my cousin, my brother, my cousin, and I against strangers."

These kinship feelings are crucial not just to our survival but also to the survival of copies of our genes that reside in our kin. We evolved to favor those with our genes over those without.

Religions evoke and exploit kin emotions. Roman Catholicism offers a superb example. The nuns are "sisters" or even "mother superiors," the priests are "fathers," the monks are "brothers," the Pope is the "Holy Father," and the religion itself is referred to as the "Holy Mother Church."

Exploitation of kin emotions is central to the recruitment and training of today's male suicide bombers and submission to the group and its god. Kinship cues are manipulated. Charismatic recruiters and trainers create cells of fictive kin, pseudobrothers outraged at the treatment of their Muslim brothers and sisters and separated from actual kin. The appeal of such martyrdom is not just the sexual fantasy of multiple heavenly virgins, but the chance to give chosen kin punched tickets to paradise.

A June 18, 2010, report from the Associated Press powerfully illustrates kinship use by religion: "an Al-Qaeda-linked insurgent shot and killed his own father as he slept in his bed for refusing to quit his job as an Iraqi interpreter for the U.S. military." In this situation, the extraordinary power of created religious "kinship" trumped actual kinship, overriding not just individual kinship emotions but a general cultural taboo against patricide. This shows how genuinely dangerous religions can become.

And the largest single loss of American civilian life in a nonnatural disaster until the events of 9/11 came about because of religion, when a total of 918 people died at Jonestown—909 of them by suicide, with some killing their own children before drinking a cyanide-laced punch. The community was founded by Jim Jones, the charismatic "father" of the People's Temple, a religious cult he created.

Why did those 909 people trust a madman with their lives?

Costly Signaling

How do you trust a person who promises to do something? Your trust rises if the promise comes with a hard-to-fake, honest, *costly signal of commitment*: a $1,000 up-front down payment; a diamond ring; self-flagellation in the name of a god; uprooting yourself and your congregation or family to create an entirely new town in Central America.

Hard-to-fake, honest, costly signals of commitment are part of our relationships. Religions use these quite nicely. They entice us to commit to them and to sacrifice our blood, sweat, toils, tears, spare change, great fortunes, and even our own kin.

How do I judge your commitment to the faith and to me as a brother in the faith? I watch your hard-to-fake, costly participation in the rituals of our faith—rituals that are often long, tedious, uncomfortable, and financially and physically taxing.

8

Wherever Two or More
of You Are Gathered
Harnessing Brain Chemistry through Ritual

The formation of different languages and of distinct species and the proofs that both have been developed through a gradual process, are curiously parallel.

—Charles Darwin

Like religious ideas and beliefs, religious rituals are by-products of mental mechanisms originally designed for other purposes.

Rituals maintain, transmit, and propagate belief across time and space. We have seen how vulnerable the individual mind is to generating, accepting, and believing religious ideas. If the process stopped there, religious beliefs might be loosely held. But, by mobilizing powerful brain chemicals that arouse intense emotional experiences and give rise to feelings as diverse as self-esteem, pleasure, fear, motivation, pain relief, and attachment, ritual creates a whole far stronger than the sum of its parts. The group nature of ritual takes individual minds already primed for belief and throws them into a continuous loop of mutual reinforcement, creating a volatile congregation of conscious and unconscious forces.

In a sense there is only one real religion, created by our hunter-gatherer ancestors, the original *Homo sapiens* in Africa, some 50,000 to 70,000 years ago. Our window into deep time, when these rituals were created, comes from three surviving populations of hunter-gatherers.

First are the Kung San of Africa, who until recently lived a hunter-gatherer lifestyle. Second is a tribe that lived isolated from the world until the twentieth century in the Bay of Bengal's Andaman Islands; its members are thought to be descended from the original band of humans who left Africa, traveled south around the Arabian Peninsula, then around India, and ultimately to Indonesia and Australia. Third are the Australian aborigines, who, according to genetic evidence, came from Africa in one wave.

All three of these tribes have religions that are striking in their similarity. They are all based on song, dance, and trance. Why? It turns out those are activities that harness some of our most powerful brain chemicals, the ones that influence pleasure, fear, love, trust, self-esteem, and attachment. So powerful was the religion our ancestors discovered that if you look closely, you still see echoes of this first religion in all of the faiths on the planet today. Just as we are all the sons and daughters of that small band of hunter-gatherers that roamed

Africa less than a hundred thousand years ago, so too are all our religions derivative of their discovery of the power of song, dance, and trance.

The Brain Chemistry of Ritual

Cells within the brain communicate through neurotransmitters, allowing signals to move from cell to cell.

Every animal with a central nervous system has *serotonin*, the oldest of a class of neurotransmitters called monoamines. Serotonin neurons reside in the brain stem and send projections throughout the brain for a variety of reasons, including gross and repetitive motor movement. But more important to this topic is that serotonin also chemically regulates our self-esteem in accord with social feedback.

If I am fired from all of my jobs, my serotonin levels and activity will decrease, and the loss in social standing likely will trigger depression, irritability, and impulsivity in me. Conversely, if you, the reader, are made president of the United States, whether or not you want the job, your serotonin levels and activity will increase, and you will feel more esteemed. Modern antidepressants such as Prozac increase serotonin activity.

As you sit quietly reading this, the serotonin neurons in your brain stem are going about three cycles per second. If you are up, moving around, they are firing at five cycles per second. When you do heavy exercise, you receive a boost in serotonin.

Another monoamine neurotransmitter of some renown is *dopamine*, generally associated with pleasure. A dopamine-rich area of our brain called the nucleus accumbens lights up with pleasure in response to certain stimuli, such as food, sex, and drugs. This is what triggers the "do-it-again" response to fast food.

Yet dopamine is more than just the pleasure chemical. Dopamine is involved with muscle function, fine motor movement, repetitive compulsive behavior, and perseveration, the uncontrollable repetition of a certain response. It was a dopamine analog that temporarily revived catatonic patients being treated by neuroscientist Oliver Sacks, who recorded the phenomenon in his 1973 book, *Awakenings*, later fictionalized in a 1990 film of the same name. Dopamine also helps to mark things in our brains as important, to give them salience, and to anticipate a reward.

The last of the monoamine neurotransmitters are *epinephrine* and *norepinephrine*, better known as adrenaline and noradrenaline. Adrenaline increases our heart rates, makes us feel anxious, focuses our attention, and causes us to sweat. It provides temporary bursts of strength, allowing us to flee or fight, and sometimes allows otherwise impossible physical feats, such as a mother lifting a car to free her child.

Oxytocin is of particular interest in religious rituals because of its bonding properties. During childbirth, the mother's brain releases a massive dose of oxytocin in response to cervical and vaginal dilation. Breastfeeding triggers the letdown response for milk, which stimulates more oxytocin. Oxytocin loosens the mother's other attachments and helps her to focus on, commit to, and attach to the infant.

Oxytocin also increases during sexual arousal, and orgasm releases a nice hit of it.

Oxytocin generates trust, love, generosity, and empathy in both sexes. It reduces fear and probably has a positive impact on all of our social emotions. Early religions able to utilize oxytocin would have been able to insinuate themselves into the potentials for man's most powerful, pleasurable, and dangerous emotions.

The *endorphins*, the last neurochemicals of specific importance to religion, are our internal opiates; the word actually derives from the term "endogenous morphine." The endorphins' main function is to block pain when injury occurs, and they are produced by exercise, excitement, pain, touch, laughter, music, orgasm, chili peppers, and the placenta.

If a runner is put into a brain scanner after a long run, endorphin receptors light up. The increase in endorphins is what causes a "runners high," and it occurs with vigorous exercise for a reason.

For our ancestors, the reason for this endorphin rush was survival. Vigorous exercise generally signaled a substantial risk of injury, whether they were hunting or being hunted. If injury did occur, their brains were ready for it, providing a pain-relieving chemical that also allowed a sense of control and power, at least until all threats had passed. This is why today's weekend warriors can continue their activity past what would normally be a pain threshold—at least until the next day—just as their ancestors would have been safe from immediate threat.

Endorphins also facilitate social bonds and increase the release of dopamine. This is a cycle unique to neurotransmitters. Though each has a specific function, they overlap and can stimulate each other, creating unique combinations that can be exploited for specific purposes—which brings us to religious rituals.

With no knowledge of neurochemistry, somehow our ancestors stumbled upon combinations of activities that could stimulate and boost serotonin, dopamine, epinephrine, norepinephrine, oxytocin, and the endorphins, creating brain activity unique to those combinations. And that is the key to understanding the enduring place of rituals in all cultures because, literally, there is nothing else like them.

The word religion probably derives from the Latin "*religare*," which means "to bind, or tie." The religious rituals invented by our ancestors captured our chemistry in a singular, uniquely human way that tied people together and facilitated social bonds.

To survive in a hostile environment, our ancestors established social groups, which created a new set of problems. Groups experienced interpersonal differences and disputes, which could doom the group if not resolved. But within a species as social as we are, anarchy was not an evolutionary option. If one member acted in a way inimical to group survival, an individual or subgroup that dared to discipline that member risked revenge from the offenders' friends or kin. But unseen forces—dead ancestors or gods—could determine punishment and reinforce groupishness easily and with constant vigilance.

Recent research supports this hypothesis. In a study about the effects of religion on punishment, Ryan McKay and his colleagues in Zurich, Switzerland, and England have demonstrated that participants who were given subliminal religious suggestions (religious priming) when determining punishment of unfair behavior in others tended to punish more severely than others. Participants were subliminally primed with religious primes, secular punishment primes, or control primes. Religion increased costly punishment, clearly trumping the other two groups. Two mechanisms were operative. The first was a "supernatural watcher" mechanism. Religious participants punish unfair behaviors when primed because they sense that failure to do so will enrage or disappoint an observing supernatural agent. The second mechanism involved the religious activation of cultural norms about fairness and its enforcement.

Thus, creation of gods or salient ancestors made eminent, if unconscious, sense, and creating rituals to help communicate with those invisible forces likely was the next logical step. But if ritual first invoked unseen and powerful others, how did our ancestors come to believe in specific invisible deities, or accept that dead ancestors could still hold power?

Well, we are brought back to the building blocks of belief—the perception of a power higher than ourselves, the sense of being able to communicate or interact with that power, and so on.

Then, as now, god was a product of the mind—or, more precisely, a by-product of the mind's cognitive mechanisms.

The Role of Dreams in Ritual—and Trance

Our ancestors most likely literally dreamed up gods. Today, we know that *dreams* are a product of our brains; that they might provide insight into our emotional lives, and we accept that they may or may not make sense. Freud called dreams the "royal road to the unconscious."

But as far as we know, our deep ancestral societies did not include skilled therapists, and even the best scientists and therapists today cannot be entirely sure how or why we dream the things we dream. But our ancestors dreamed, too, and we have reason to believe that they believed that dreams were uniquely powerful.

Beginning in the fifth century BCE, the ancient Greeks, a relatively recent and enlightened civilization, built incubation centers, temples dedicated to Asclepius, the god of healing. Citizens would go to the temples to sleep and induce dreams through ritual, fasting, and prayer, using information from dreams for healing and believing that the gods revealed themselves in dreams. The early Egyptians also saw dreams as a key source of divine information.

Go back further in human development, and imagine a hunter-gatherer asleep on the plains of Africa ten millennia ago, visited in sleep by a deceased relative in a dream that made no apparent sense. It would seem logical to accept the odd landscapes of dreams as an invisible reality, perhaps another world filled with wiser and more powerful ancestral spirits or some sorts of deities that could offer guidance.

Combine that with a sense of wonder at the natural world, mix in decoupled cognition, which as already demonstrated allows us to accept unseen beings, and we could have the beginnings of gods.

We will never know exactly how our remote ancestors created the first gods. Gods may have been created also as personifications and explanations of natural forces such as fire, which is still present in rituals for most of the world's religions, in the form of candles. Imagine our ancestors harnessing fire for the first time. It must have seemed truly miraculous. Combine that with dramatic weather changes, volcanoes, the sun, the moon, and other natural wonders. As with all other powerful psychological phenomena, there were undoubtedly multiple determinants of those first supernatural beings.

With the beginnings of gods probably came the beginnings of a desire to communicate with them, to reach them at will, not just during sleep. Like their ancient Greek descendants, if our ancestors wanted to deliberately commune with that dream world, rather than rely on chance encounters in sleep, they had to build their own "royal road." So it's very possible that they learned, as closely as possible, to create trance, a waking, deliberate dream state, through dance, drumming, and singing for hours or days on end. Much like certain Native American cultures, they might have isolated themselves and experienced sensory deprivation causing them to sense the presence of another, feeling at one with everything. Fasting can disturb perceptions and even cause hallucinations. Most religions embrace fasting, perhaps for its vision-enhancing effects. And as our ancestors created these rituals over time, they learned to boost those neurotransmitters and create the biotechnology of group cohesion.

It is also likely that our hyperactive agency detection device, mentioned earlier, which tends to ascribe human agency to abstract sights or sounds, was turbocharged by neurochemicals during ritual, predisposing our ancestors to believe not only in invisible ancestors but also in other humanlike entities.

Early rituals centered on activities or things that we now know can alter brain chemistry: music, song, intense rhythmic activity, and strong emotion, combined with sleep deprivation. Many rituals were literally exhaustive, with people dancing and singing all night or longer. Such intense, prolonged activity brought brain chemicals to peak activity.

Our ancestors likely found that dance (and possibly that certain substances) induced trance and that ritual allowed for what seemed to be deliberate access to the unseen beings. It also was a public validation of the existence of another world, and the invisible spirits within it. Consider how the word "enthusiasm" derives from the Greek "*enthousiasmos*," which means "possessed by God."

During ritual, focus was on the community, not the individual, and the rituals could create and convey morals or lessons important to the group's survival. The rituals accomplished what individuals could not: they could evoke a world of unseen dangers, especially from deceased ancestors, for tribe members who stepped out of line.

These early religious rituals generally marked rites of passage: birth, puberty, marriage, and death. Anthropologist Rodney Needham has noted that in today's remaining hunter-gatherer societies, percussion plays a strong role in marking life transitions. Rituals centering on transitions, marked by percussion, remain prominent in every culture to this day. Remnants survive in college fraternities, where hazing represents this tradition of terrifying, painful, and sometimes deadly initiation rites. Even a mosh pit resembles ritualistic frenzy.

All three of the surviving tribes that provide us with windows into deep time use rituals to induct men into the secrets of the tribe. Initiation rituals can be painful and terrifying, thus releasing relevant neurochemicals, and the resultant bonding strengthens the tribe. Such rituals energize men for war, make them loyal, and instill courage and attachment to conventions of the tribe.

Today's Australian aborigines call the time before history "the Dreamtime," when mythical beings roamed the country, fighting, hunting, and creating the natural world. Even today, specific rituals are generally kept secret from outsiders, continuing to create a powerful group bond. We do know that aboriginal ceremonies are long, often consisting of chanting or singing the Dreamtime myths, contemplating sacred objects, and introducing the myths and objects to initiates. The rituals include dancing and miming the actions of totemic animals, hand clapping, beating sticks or stones, and, in some parts of Australia, playing didgeridoos.

Ritual as Survival Mechanism

Our ancestors' *religious rituals* solved several problems at once. A group could evoke punishment for wrongdoers, resolve conflict, identify free riders, settle feuds, wipe the slate clean, and create an arena in which hard-to-fake, costly, honest signals could be received and scrutinized. Rituals may have even solved a very simple survival problem by frightening away predators.

These early religions had probably no priests or ecclesiastical hierarchy. There may have been alpha males or elders who created quasi-leadership positions, which later led to shamanism, but corporeal messengers from the unseen, separate priestly "professions" resembling modern-day clergy, likely did not exist.

As Nicholas Wade notes in his book *The Faith Instinct*, the rituals generate an intense sense of togetherness and awe, and a desire to put the group's interest above the personal, "it ties a clever knot." We lose our sense of self and become deeply bonded to those we touch and with whom we sing and dance throughout a long night.

The archaeological and anthropological record supports the conclusion that our hunter-gatherer ancestors maintained these rituals wherever they migrated. Their portable, enduring rituals continued to center on song, dance, and trance.

Settled societies emerged 15,000 years ago; 10,000 years ago marked the invention of agriculture. Though today there are few if any true hunter-gatherers, the religion created by our hunter-gatherer ancestors had become too powerful to be discarded, so as we adapted, so did religion.

Humanity became essentially agrarian. Religion took on the rhythm of the seasons, so important to agriculture, and we see that legacy to this day. Paganism and pantheism created Oestra, the spring festival. In Judaism, Sukkoth marks the end of the food harvest. Passover is the beginning of the barley festival. Shavu'ot marks the end of the wheat harvest. Christianity incorporated these rituals into Easter and other holidays.

With the emergence of literate societies approximately 5,000 years ago, access to the supernatural was no longer a democratic undertaking. Priestly castes, allied with political power, put on constraints. And the priests or shamans learned that they had power without responsibility—that they could blame failures on deities already firmly entrenched, for which they claimed to be the mere messenger.

The earliest rituals of song, dance, and trance were social levelers, bringing a community together and overriding whatever hierarchy existed. The move toward settled societies and civilization created greater social stratification. In some religions, dancing, with its social equality creating effects, was ultimately banished—but rhythmic movement has been maintained. Look no further than the coordinated prayers in Islam, masses of men, lined up symmetrically, kneeling and prostrating themselves in unison, a kind of floor dance. Or go to a Roman Catholic mass and watch the genuflection before the altar, the alternating of kneeling, sitting, and standing during a mass, and consider the role of Gregorian chant in the church's Latin rituals as recently as the 1960s. Look at the power of Gospel music in traditionally African-American churches, with roots in African dance and ritual.

In other religions, we see the power of rituals primarily because they are so feared. Some Southern Baptists never make love standing up so that God does not think they are dancing. Pews in Christian churches did not start out as seating; that was an afterthought. Pews were originally placed in European churches in the sixteenth century to prevent dancing. They remain but often fail to constrain worshippers in some of the more demonstrative congregations.

For our ancestors, singing and dancing, music and movement, were all one.

Music's origins are still debated. Is it a by-product of other mechanisms, hard vowels and consonants originally put to the rhythm of a beating heart? Or is music an actual stand-alone adaptation? Darwin thought that music was one of the best examples of his idea of sexual selection.

"I conclude that musical notes and rhythm were first acquired by the male or female progenitors of mankind for the sake of charming the opposite sex. The musical tones became firmly associated with some of the strongest passions an animal is capable of feeling." Darwin noted that many of the emotions induced by music have to do with love.

This points to another aspect of the original religious rituals. Consider them an early version of the Saturday night square dance, a place to look for and assess potential mates. What better way to gauge strength, coordination, character, commitment to the group, and others' view of an individual you fancied? Singing, dancing, and trancing are hard-to-fake, honest signals of "mate-worthiness."

Precaution

You certainly have seen a Catholic athlete step to the line to start a race and cross himself. It is an appeal to a god and an ease to anxiety. The basketball star, Lebron James, goes through a ritual before the start of every game. He pours talcum powder on his hands, claps them, with powder spraying everywhere, and then throws the remainder in the air toward cheering fans, a nice boost of reassurance and anxiety reduction. Such repetitive obsessional actions serve as a means of allaying fear.

Sigmund Freud thought that religion was society's obsessive-compulsive disorder and that obsessive-compulsive disorder was an individual's private religion. He saw the link but did not have the tools to fully understand it. We now know that the brain has *precautionary vigilance systems* that can be triggered to take repetitive or stereotyped action to allay anxiety. These same mechanisms are used in religious ritual and help allay the anxiety generated by uncertainty or risk, both inherent to life, but especially so in the harsh, dangerous world of our ancestors.

Synchrony and Union

Religious rituals utilize our mirror neurons, which will be discussed more fully in chapter 9. The original purpose of these mirror neurons probably was to help prepare an organism to learn and make new movements. Religious rituals take advantage of this. It is hard not to dance when people around you are dancing, and the mirror neurons make it easier to do so in coordinated *synchrony*. Research at Stanford Business School has shown that merely engaging in a synchronous activity, even without heavy muscle involvement, will enhance cooperation and the feelings that accompany it. There is a difference in how you feel about others when you are strolling as a group or walking, still relaxed, in lock step with them.

Throw in heavy muscle activity and it rises to another level. If the synchronous movement involves vigorous muscle activity, pain thresholds actually rise. A novel experiment at Oxford University compared rowers working together and alone on rowing machines. When the experiment was controlled for the amount of work output, it became clear that an individual rowing with others at the same output level had a higher pain threshold than when the individual worked equally hard alone. Endorphins rise with group activity. And we know that endorphins enhance social bonds.

Consider Woodstock, a defining moment not just for the people who were there but for an entire generation. That event is noteworthy for its lack of violence and conflict, for its masses of people united under adverse conditions, working together, celebrating youth with music, dance, sex, camaraderie, and, yes, mind-altering drugs, mere supplements to the brain chemistry that the atmosphere and synchrony would have themselves triggered.

We even see the bonding power of ritual in something as simple, all-American, and ubiquitous as the high school pep rally, designed to unite the entire student population to oppose the rival.

The Magic of Touch

Primates spend a seemingly inordinate amount of time grooming each other, probably for reasons beyond health or parasite removal. The evidence suggests that *touch* stimulates oxytocin to initiate social bonding, and then endorphins to strengthen it.

If you show a woman a threat scenario when she is not holding someone's hand, her amygdala, the part of the brain that controls fear, will really light up. She is afraid. If she is holding a stranger's hand, the fear is somewhat eased. If she is holding her partner's hand, it is eased even more. What is more remarkable is that the degree to which a partner's hand calms fear is directly proportional to how the woman rates the quality of the relationship. A good partnership calms fear better than a less good one.

With touch, those prefrontal areas of our brain that regulate emotion relax and allow us to focus on problem solving. The brain processes a supportive touch as a signal another person will share the load. Humans are the most cooperative primate species, and touch helps build those problem-solving relationships across the brains of our allies.

Another piece of research shows that basketball teams that touch the most do the best. All those high fives, chest bumps, butt slaps, and contact after a successful shot or between foul shots translates into boosts of neurotransmitters that enhance cooperative feelings, solidarity, and group cohesion.

Once our ancestors, however inadvertently, learned to create the chemistry that augments trust, love, cooperation, and selflessness, there was no turning back. Inevitably, those incredibly powerful chemical reactions supercharged the cognitive mechanisms that permit supernatural belief, and religion was launched.

A Little Experiment

Take a moment. Think of someone you like or love, and consider your feelings for that person. Now do a brief assessment of your own emotional state at this instant. Then pinch some skin on your hand until it hurts.

Once you have made those three measurements, stand and belt out a song while you sway back and forth and move in rhythm to your voice. If there is someone with you, put your arms around each other's shoulders and sway as the two of you sing. When you finish, after any awkward feeling has cleared, repeat the measurements. See where your pain threshold is when you pinch your skin. How are you feeling about that someone? How are you feeling about yourself? (You may ignore how the neighbor who just saw you doing this through your window may be perceiving you.)

When I do this with audiences, almost everyone reports positive changes in several of the parameters. (Imagine atheist audiences belting out four stanzas of "Amazing Grace.") In this short exercise, you will get a little taste of the neurochemical changes triggered by song, touch, and rhythmic movement. And that is only after a few moments. Imagine doing it all night on the savannahs of Africa or in the outback of Australia.

If you have ever gone to a rock concert, where fans stand, sway, sing along, and hold up lighters, or, more recently, cell phones, and left the concert feeling exhilarated and renewed, you have felt the power of ritual and touch.

Rituals serve as displays of "mate-worthiness," and this touches on two other aspects of our humanity utilized by religion.

Romantic Love

Our romantic relationships are served by specific adaptations in our brain. Sexual desire puts us on the playing field; *romantic love* solves the problem of committing strongly to one person. Religion often taps into this and creates a love relationship. It is reflected in the promise to Muslim martyrs that in heaven they shall be married. The late Sheikh Yassin, Hamas's spiritual adviser, said that it was okay for women to be suicide bombers, particularly if they were single, because they become "even more beautiful than the seventy-two virgins. . . . they are guaranteed a pure husband in Paradise." The promise of seventy-two virgins to male suicide martyrs probably is more lasciviousness than romance, capitalizing on males' endless libido focused on young fertile women.

Capacities for romantic love are extensively utilized in religion. Consider Mother Teresa's recently published letters, in which she speaks of being married to Christ. In fact, in medieval times, nuns' consecration ceremonies were, essentially, weddings—complete with dowries for the church. Even today, many orders of nuns call themselves "brides of Christ," and some take their final vows in wedding dresses, and receive and wear wedding rings.

In a delightful one-woman show called *Letting Go of God*, the one-time *Saturday Night Live* comedian Julia Sweeney reveals that, in her youth, a painting of Jesus helped her relieve her sexual longings.

The attachment system, discussed in chapter 3, is deeply involved in our romantic relationships. We go from desire to intense romantic infatuation to companionate love, with the last stage based on the attachment system.

Parental Investment
The primary behavior difference between the sexes is not entirely determined by the genetic sex. Instead, it is determined by behavior called *parental investment*, which reflects which sex has the biggest physiological stake in the offspring, and thus the biggest emotional investment.

In most sexual species, the female has the greatest parental investment. In ours, for instance, the woman has to produce a viable nutrient-rich egg, for which her uterus prepares every nonpregnant month of her reproductive life, gestate a fetus for nine months, go through the potentially fatal process of childbirth, and lactate for months if not years. The basic physiologic cost is enormous. In the males of our species the minimum cost is sperm and five minutes.

That is a considerable discrepancy in parental investment at just the physiological level. After a child is born, even in "progressive" Western cultures the greatest responsibility for physical and emotional care falls on the woman. Fathers might change diapers now and again, but it is still most likely to be the mother's domain.

Behaviorally, the sex with the greatest parental investment is choosy about whom she, and it is usually a she, mates with. She is the rate-limiting step in reproduction. The sex with the least parental investment, usually the male, must compete fiercely with other members of his sex to gain access to the female and to ensure survival of his DNA.

In humans, this biologically based female importance and choosiness seems to have acted as an affront to males, who constantly devise ways to control female reproduction. Tactics include everything from polygamy to insisting that women wear head-to-toe black covering, and even to more brutal practices like clitoridectomies and infibulations. In some civil wars, which may be religion- or sect-based, men show triumph over enemies by raping their foes' women while the vanquished are forced to watch mute and helpless. This is considered more of an affront to the men than to "their" women, who nonetheless may bear a lifetime stigma, even among their own people. The same stigmatized fate may befall any resulting offspring.

And religious belief appears to be an important factor in our culture of monogamy-based relationships, which by definition results in more competition among both sexes to secure a suitable mate. Consider the traditional Christian wedding ceremony: "What God hath joined together, let no man set asunder."

A 2009 study of Arizona college students showed that both men and women appeared to have an increase in religious feelings when shown pictures of attractive members of their own sex—not, as you might think, attractive members of the opposite sex. Thus, when competitiveness for potential mates comes into play, so does religion.

Most religions are preoccupied with sex, and that in itself offers strong evidence that religion is man-made.

Up to this point we have described the basic psychological building blocks of belief and ritual—how it is a by-product of adaptive cognitive mechanisms. But, we also now possess evidence from imaging studies of our brains. Let's now look at what is seen through that window into the mind.

9

Oh Ye of Little Faith
Discovering the Physical Evidence of God(s) as By-product

> *How paramount the future is to the present when one is surrounded by children.*
>
> —Charles Darwin

The word by-product sounds trivial, as if it means weakness, or insignificance. Quite the contrary. Reading and writing, for instance, are cultural by-products of adaptations originally designed for other purposes. We do not have reading and writing modules in our brain. What we do have is vision, a spoken language, symbolic thought, and fine motor movement of our hands, along with various other adaptations originally designed for other purposes. All of these adaptations came together when humans created writing and reading, the most important cultural invention of our species.

Similarly, music possibly is a by-product of spoken language, with its hard vowels and consonants, put to rhythm, originally the rhythm of a beating heart. To appreciate a cultural by-product's power to move us, just listen to a favorite piece of music, especially one that evokes memories.

Religion is a powerful force that has shaped history and individual behavior beyond measure. Calling it a by-product does not diminish its obvious power, especially when recent respected studies support it as such. Recent revealing and powerful empirical evidence now exists to explain religion's supernormal power over us.

As Lone Frank, the Danish neurobiologist and journalist says, "the sacred is found between the ears." And, with the new techniques of neuroscience and imaging, that is exactly what is being discovered.

Probably the most famous in this new world of brain research and religion has been Michael Persinger, a psychologist at Laurentian University in Canada. Since the 1980s he has experimented with what is now known as the "God Helmet." People are placed in a dark and quiet room, sight and sound perception are blocked, and a helmet that magnetically stimulates the temporal lobes is placed over the head.

Test subjects report the presence of "another." Depending on their personal and cultural history, the "sensed presence" might be interpreted by the helmeted subject to be a supernatural religious figure. Women reported these experiences more frequently than men.

Persinger argues that we do not have a stable, single sense of self or one part of the brain from which it emanates. There are instead several areas of the brain that contribute to our conscious experience of our self. In our usual waking state, the left side of our brain, which controls language, dominates. In other settings, such as those marked by fear, depression, personal crisis, too little oxygen, low blood sugar, or the wearing of the "God Helmet," when the right temporal area is stimulated, that additional sense of self intrudes into consciousness and feels like "another."

This stimulation of religious experiences via the temporal lobes is not just an academic oddity or artifact of magnets in a lab. The temporal lobes are crucial for speech, and a common element of religious experiences is hearing the voice of a god. One can misattribute our inner voice to an outsider's voice. It has been documented for years that many individuals with temporal lobe epilepsy, which comes from electrical disturbances in the temporal lobes, have intense religious experiences, and that extreme religiosity is a common character trait among such patients.

It is possible that St. Paul was actually having an epileptic fit when he was "struck down" on the road to Damascus, and equally possible—even likely—that some of the founders and leaders of the world's various religions would today be evaluated and treated for temporal lobe epilepsy. Saint Teresa of Avila, Feodor Dostoevsky, and Marcel Proust, among others, are thought to have had temporal lobe epilepsy, which may have contributed to their focus on the spiritual.

Andrew Newberg, MD, an internist and radiologist at Thomas Jefferson University Hospital and Medical College and an adjunct professor in the Department of Religious Studies at the University of Pennsylvania, pioneered neuroimaging studies of nuns praying, monks meditating, Pentecostals speaking in tongues, and individuals in various trance states. His work suggests that emotional states in which the individual "feels at one with the universe" correspond to high frontal lobe activity and low activity in the brain's left parietal lobe, an area responsible for integrating information that orients us in our environment. That area tells us where our body ends and the world begins.

If sensory input to that region of the brain is blocked by intense prayer, meditation, slow chanting, elegiac melodies, whispered ritual incantations, or other techniques, the brain may be prevented from distinguishing self and nonself, inner and outer world. When that area does not integrate such information from the outside world, the individual will feel merged into everything.

Admittedly, such studies involve exceptions—helmeted subjects, nuns, epileptics, mystics, Pentecostals, and others on the extremes. For example, when Pentecostals and Charismatic Christians speak in tongues, glossolalia, the opposite happens. There is low frontal lobe activity, which corresponds with feeling a loss of control, and high parietal activity, which corresponds with an intense experience of the self in relation to a god, an attachment figure.

With regard to modern neuroimaging investigations in more ordinary religious and nonreligious folks, "The Cognitive and Neural Foundations of Religious Belief," a study published in the spring of 2009 from the National Institutes of Health by Dimitrios Kapogiannis and five other researchers, gives us stunning evidence to support the by-product theory of religion.

Test subjects' brains were monitored using functional magnetic resonance imaging (fMRI). While researchers read to them various statements about religion, subjects were asked to agree or disagree. Although no "god center" was found within the brain, the neuroimaging evidence did localize religious belief within the same brain networks that process capacities for theory of mind, intent, and emotion.

A comparison of results from both religious and nonreligious test subjects revealed no differences in the brain mechanisms used to assess the statements. Religiosity is not a separate function; it is integrated into the same brain networks used in social cognition. Religious belief is not sui generis—not unique. The study provides powerful evidence that religious beliefs engage well-known, ordinary, social brain circuits and mind mechanisms, and that these mechanisms mediate the adaptive functions already described herein.

Another recent study by Sam Harris also used fMRI and tested both religious believers and nonbelievers as they were presented with religious and nonreligious propositions. The believers' brains showed activity in parts having to do with identity and with how the individual both sees and represents himself, regardless of the content presented to them.

Mirror Neurons

Mirror neurons, which exist in all of our brains, probably in many different areas, were discovered accidentally by researchers working with Macaque monkeys at the University of Parma in the 1980s and 1990s. Subsequent research has shown them to be active in humans as well. Their discovery is one of the most important recent findings in neuroscience. These neurons fire both when an animal performs an action and when the animal observes the same action done by another animal. These neurons "mirror" the behavior of the other, as if the observer were performing the same action. So it really is true that "monkey see, monkey do."

Let's illustrate this. When you raise your right hand, nerve cells activate on the left side of your brain, in the area that controls right-arm movement. If you watch me do this, the same neurons will light up, even though your right arm remains still. If I stick a knife in my right hand, the pain per-ceiving areas of my left brain activate. If you see me do it, your brain reacts the same way.

But you do not need pain to prove this to yourself. If you watch someone suck on a lemon wedge, you will "taste" the bitter lemon and your mouth will water, just as if you were doing it yourself. Or try not to yawn when someone else does.

Fundraisers understand this at some level. They can recite all the statistics about child hunger in the world without much effect on the typical person, but if they show that person a picture of one starving child, he or she will be much more likely to donate. The 2010 earthquake in Haiti released a massive outpouring from around the world due to the horrific images and stories flashed across the media. We all could feel the pain of loss and hopelessness, and our heartstrings would not allow us to sit by and do nothing.

We often hear that if it weren't for religion, we would be immoral and unethical. Mirror neurons resoundingly refute this. We literally feel other's pain, and that induces in us empathy, distress, and the urge to help. Our brains are ethical by design. Religions utilize this, and, consciously or not, they utilize it in a way that can traumatize.

How many children are exposed to the distressing image of the crucifixion? Most Christians may think they have become used to it, but the evidence would suggest that every time they see it, at some level they still feel that pain, as if they were being nailed to the cross. That image is a very powerful manipulator of our basic ethical capacities.

Mel Gibson, the famously "traditionalist" Roman Catholic actor and director, took full-out advantage of this tendency in his 2004 film *The Passion of the Christ*, which is so graphically violent that even some Christians blanched. Gibson was accused of both anti-Semitism and of prolonging the film's violence for the express purpose of strengthening religious belief. The film spawned two documentaries and still has an active Web site that makes the film available—with added violence cut from the film's theater release—as teaching tools for churches.

Some zealously religious people reportedly have, over the life of Christianity, even physically manifested the stigmata—the mysterious appearance on their hands, feet, and side of the wounds of Christ's crucifixion. They are generally designated as saints, but it is more likely that their unconscious mind perceived that image so powerfully and so traumatically that it was physically manifested. This kind of mind power is not unknown to science. It is equally likely that they inflicted wounds to themselves while in a trancelike state, either knowingly or unknowingly.

As you read this there are dedicated researchers at work who continue to harness modern neuroscience to explore how our brains generate, accept, and spread religious beliefs. They will build on the work just described and one day they will give us a comprehensive neuroanatomy of religious belief in the brain. Count on it.

10

Lest Ye Be Judged
Educating Our Minds

Ignorance more frequently begets confidence than does knowledge: it is those who know little, and not those who know much, who so positively assert that this or that problem will never be solved by science.

—Charles Darwin

In 1918 William Jennings Bryan, former secretary of state and presidential candidate, began what Dudley Malone called his "duel to the death with evolution." The battle culminated in the summer of 1925 with the famous Scopes Trial in Dayton, Tennessee. But it was not evolution that died. Clarence Darrow, the lead defense attorney, called Bryan to the stand as a hostile witness, then demolished Bryan's foolish biblical literalism point by point. It ranks as one of the great cross-examinations in American legal history. Bryan had to know he had been humiliated; he died five days later.

Although John Scopes, who taught evolution in a high school, was convicted of violating Tennessee's Butler Act, which expressly forbade the teaching of evolution, the conviction was later overturned and the case was not retried. So though Bryan technically won the court fight, he inevitably lost the battle.

The broader war, however, is not over. The Butler Act actually remained in effect for almost forty years and the legal issues surrounding the teaching of evolution remained dormant until another teacher challenged the act on First Amendment grounds in 1967.

Since the mid-1960s, there have been nineteen major challenges to the teaching of evolution, two before the United States Supreme Court. Many in the religious right have tried to derail the teaching of evolution by insisting that creation science and its most recent version, intelligent design, be taught side by side with Darwinian evolution. But every time the issue has reached a decisive point in our legal system, science has won.

As recently as late 2005, Judge John E. Jones III, a Pennsylvania federal district court judge, ruled against requiring the presentation of intelligent design as an alternative to Darwinian evolution in ninth-grade science classes. In *Kitzmiller v. Dover Area School District*, Kenneth Miller, a Brown University biologist and practicing Catholic, testified in support of the scientific integrity of evolution, stating that there is no conflict between religion and science. His words echoed the most famous speech from the Scopes Trial, the "academic freedom" speech by Clarence Darrow's co-counsel, Dudley Malone, who noted no conflict between evolution science and religion. While the Dover case marked a great victory for science and science education, Judge Jones, in an otherwise exemplary decision, conformed to the viewpoint of Miller and Malone, making explicit reference to this presumed absence of conflict between science and religion.

Despite the political correctness of proclaiming no conflict between science and religion, the constant din of battles in school boards and educational committees across the United States (and, more recently, in the United Kingdom and Canada) is becoming deafening. There unquestionably *is* a conflict between religion and science.

For centuries religious dogma has made claims about the origins of the cosmos, the origins and nature of man, and the nature of the universe. Science has slowly but irrefutably disproved these claims and explanations, not without peril, as Galileo might tell you were he still living. The real search for truth shows that men and women in today's world are an African ape, the last surviving hominid, *Homo sapiens*.

As we noted in chapter 3, even Darwin had difficulty abandoning religion, and he had only a fraction of empirical evidence to consider, compared to what we now know.

The mental mechanisms that combine to make us vulnerable to religious belief are deeply ingrained. When they combine with societal indoctrination of children, *often* from birth, we face what might be the ultimate battle between unquestioned belief and intelligent inquiry. As Jerry Coyne, an evolutionary biologist and former believer, has said, "In religion faith is a virtue; in science it's a vice."

It is also, as any former believer might tell you, so much easier to believe. Religions offer sets of rules and, when combined with all of our adaptive mental mechanisms, eliminates the need for serious thought about the issue. The 2010 Pew Poll on Religion actually found that agnostics and atheists were more knowledgeable about the world's religions than believers were, which would seem to indicate a higher level of thought about the issues involved.

But there is hope. In a June 6, 2010, ABC News interview, physicist Steven Hawking, considered by many to be one of the greatest scientific minds of our or any time, said, "There is a fundamental difference between religion, which is based on authority; and science, which is based on observation and reason. Science will win because it works." As most people know, without the aid of science, Hawking would long ago have succumbed to the ravages of amyotrophic lateral sclerosis (ALS, or "Lou Gehrig's disease") no matter how many people prayed for him. Instead his fine mind survives and continues to learn and teach, aided by an array of technological accoutrements.

As demonstrated in this book, science—specifically the cognitive and social neurosciences—shows us how and why human minds generate religious beliefs. More than an outline is apparent, and with each passing day, the psychological mechanisms, the neuroanatomy, and the neurochemistry of religion continue to come into sharper focus.

It will not be long before another John or Jane Scopes teaches the evolutionary cognitive neuroscience of religion in a public high school biology or psychology class. When those classes are taught, you can bet on the response by the fundamentalist Christians in the United States. They will take it to court. The case will ultimately be heard in a federal court, maybe even the Supreme Court. We should all welcome such a trial. It will generate an even wider audience for these discoveries about how human minds create and sustain religious belief. If history is any guide, science—in this case, the evolutionary cognitive neuroscience of religious belief—will win decisively.

Religion may offer comfort in a harsh world; it may foster community; it may incite conflict. In short, it may have its uses—for good and for evil. But it was created by human beings, and this will be a better world if we cease confusing it with fact.

Notes

Front cover

This NASA photo of the Helix nebula is a color-enhanced composite of images taken from the Hubble telescope and Kitt Peak National Observatory in Arizona. When it first appeared as NASA's "astronomy photo of the day" on May 10, 2003, it generated a number of e-mail chains designating it as the "Eye of God," with some claiming that seeing the image had resulted in miracles.

Preface

For my papers and presentation on suicide terrorism, see my Web site, www.jandersonthomson.com. The idea that anything we do to loosen religion's hold on humanity is a blow for civilization comes from remarks by the physicist Steven Weinberg at the Beyond Belief Symposium held in San Diego in 2006. That symposium is a rich source for talks, and I especially recommend the presentation on the unintelligent design of the universe by astrophysicist and director of the Hayden Planetarium at the American Museum of Natural History, Neil deGrasse Tyson.

Chapter 1

"Darwin's theory of evolution by natural selection is the only workable explanation that has ever been proposed for the remarkable fact of our own existence, indeed the existence of all life wherever it may turn up in the universe. It is the only known explanation for the rich diversity of animals, plants, fungi and bacteria. . . Natural selection is the only workable explanation for the beautiful and compelling illusion of 'design' that pervades every living body and every organ. Knowledge of evolution may not be strictly useful in everyday commerce. You can live some sort of life and die without ever hearing the name of Darwin. But if, before you die, you want to understand why you lived in the first place, Darwinism is the one subject that you must study." Richard Dawkins, foreword to John Maynard Smith's *The Theory of Evolution*, Canto ed. (Cambridge: Cambridge University Press, 1993).

The summary statement of evolution as an integrated collection of problem solving devices comes from Donald Symons, "Adaptationism and Human Mating Psychology," in *The Handbook of Evolutionary Psychology*, ed. David M. Buss (Hoboken, NJ: John Wiley & Sons, 2005). "The mind is what the brain does" and the analogy with the Apollo spacecraft come from Steven Pinker's *How The Mind Works* (New York: Norton, 1997).

Belief in one or more central holy figures: Although Catholicism and similar Greek and Eastern Orthodox religions are viewed primarily as monotheistic religions, they actually operate as polytheistic religions. Saints as supernatural agents provide nice proof of religion being man-made. If Catholics are honest with themselves, they'd see all of the saints as minor gods. You pray to St. Anthony if you lose something and St. Jude if you need something impossible. St. Clare became the patron saint of television in the 1950s due to her particular "vision." As founder (with St. Francis of Assisi) and abbess of the "poor Clares," she, in her old age, could no longer go to Christmas mass, so she reported that she saw it while she was alone, on the wall of her monastic cell.

Even though the saints do function as minor gods—there is a supernatural power imputed to them—it might be easier to think of them as heavenly lobbyists. Catholics pray to saints, but not to ask them to grant their prayers—only god can do that, they are told. Catholics are invoking access to god, asking the saints to "intercede" with god for them. That distinction, made very clear in Catholicism, cleverly gets around an accusation or appearance of polytheism. You can have your saints, but still one god (not counting the Trinity).

The process of designating someone as a saint, a holy person who should serve as a positive example, begins with the people who knew that person personally. The people then present evidence of holiness, usually first to a parish priest. The evidence for sainthood takes the form of miracles attributed to the saint-in-waiting—which, if you think about, negates the concept that the prospective saint merely asks god to perform miracles. The priest passes the information and documentation to a bishop, who sends it up the hierarchical chain to a cardinal and eventually the pope. Becoming a saint usually requires that at least three medical miracles be attributed to that person, though having died a martyr automatically takes the requirement down to two. (Try thinking of this in the context of suicide bombers of a different religion.)

The sainthood process is a classic example of religion and gods being created by man. In recent years, there have even been accusations that some popes "rushed" the sainthood process for political expediency. (*Sunday Times* [London], February 18, 2008.) And, of course, some saints, including the ever-popular St. Christopher, the patron saint of travelers whose image appears on many medals hanging from taxicab rearview mirrors, have been "de-sainted" by the Vatican, which apparently has the power both to create and negate minor gods.

This all makes Catholicism essentially the same as Hinduism, which is defined as henotheistic—involving devotion to a single god while accepting the existence of others.

Chapter 2
The lovely phrase, "We are risen apes, not fallen angels," is from William Allman's *Stone Age Present: How Evolution Has Shaped Modern Life—From Sex, Violence and Language to Emotions, Morals and Communities* (New York: Touchstone, 1994).

One of my favorite stories: A little girl came home from school after an early lesson in the evolution of humans. She asked her mother, "Do we come from apes?" The mother paused and said, "Well, in a sense. We arose from monkeys and apes." The little girl asked, "Well, where do monkeys come from?" The mother thought for a moment and replied, "The Kansas State Board of Education."

The overview of human evolution comes from Nicholas Wade's *Before the Dawn: Recovering the Lost History of Our Ancestors* (New York: Penguin Press, 2006) and Richard Potts and Christopher Sloan's *What It Means to Be Human* (Washington, DC: National Geographic Press, 2010). With Richard Dawkins, Todd Stiefel, Greg Langer, and a group from Howard University, I had the privilege of touring the new human origins exhibit at the Smithsonian in Washington, DC, with its director, Richard Potts. Later he kindly reviewed my summary of human evolution to ensure accuracy. See that exhibit if you can. It is education at its best.

We are a social species with a vastly underappreciated capacity for cooperation. See the first chapter, "Apes on a Plane," of Sarah Hrdy's book *Mothers and Others: The Evolution of Mutual Understanding* (Cambridge MA: Belknap Press of Harvard University Press, 2009). We are able to cram into a plane, help each other load luggage in the overhead storage, and tolerate difficult people and screaming babies. If such a plane were loaded with chimpanzee passengers, by the time the plane landed it would be full of bloody body parts.

I am indebted to Robin Cornwell for the idea of religion as the ultimate fast-food meal.

The notion of "do-it-again centers" of our brain comes from Terry Burnham and Jay Phelan, *Mean Genes: From Sex to Money to Food: Taming Our Primal Instincts* (New York: Penguin Press, 2000).

There is no better way to educate oneself about the theory of evolution, the modern Darwinian synthesis, and the evidence than to read—in this order—*The Blind Watchmaker* (New York: Norton, 1996), *The Selfish Gene*, 30th anniversary ed. (New York: Oxford University Press, 2006), and *The Greatest Show on Earth* (New York: Free Press, 2009), all by Richard Dawkins.

Chapter 3

The powerful description of the *Homo erectus* women surviving on the savannahs with vitamin A poisoning comes from Alan Walker and Pat Shipman's *The Wisdom of the Bones: In Search of Human Origins* (New York: Knopf, 1996). A cast of her bones can be seen in the Hall of Human Origins at the Natural History Museum in Washington, DC. The parallel of Pentecostals reaching up to a God with children reaching up to a parent was an essential insight of Lee Kirkpatrick's in developing his ideas about the deep connection between the attachment system and religion (personal communication, 2010). Also see his book *Attachment, Evolution, and the Psychology of Religion* (New York: Guilford Press, 2005). Also, see John Bowlby, *Attachment* (New York: Basic Books, 1969). Mary Ainsworth was a professor of psychology at the University of Virginia whose humanity and warmth remain vivid in my memory. An excellent introduction to Ainsworth and Bowlby's work can be found in "Becoming Attached" by Robert Karen in the *Atlantic Monthly*, which was later expanded into a book, *Becoming Attached: First Relationships and How They Shape Our Capacity to Love* (New York: Oxford University Press, 1994).

Frank Sulloway has a superb essay that maps out Charles Darwin's thinking in that crucial period in the late 1830s when Darwin discovered natural selection. See "Why Darwin Rejected Intelligent Design," in *Intelligent Thought: Science versus the Intelligent Design Movement*, ed. John Brockman New York: Vintage, 2006). The impact of Darwin losing his daughter, Annie, is beautifully told by his descendant Randal Keynes in *Annie's Box: Charles Darwin, His Daughter and Human Evolution* (London: Fourth Estate, 2001). The principal Darwin biography is Janet Browne's magisterial two volume work, *Voyaging* (New York: Knopf, 1995) and *The Power of Place* (Princeton, NJ: Princeton University Press, 2003).

Chapter 4
The insight into the mind-body split being part of the very structure of the perceptual tracks in the brain is found in Matthew Lieberman's essay, "What Makes Big Ideas Sticky?" in Max Brockman's edited volume *What's Next: Dispatches on the Future of Science* (New York: Vintage, 2009).

A summary of Jesse Bering's work and ingenious experiments is found in his article "The Cognitive Psychology of Belief in the Supernatural," in *American Scientist* 92 (2006): 142–149. He writes well, and his essays for *Scientific American Mind* are always worth reading. Be on the lookout for his book *The Belief Instinct: The Psychology of Souls, Destiny, and the Meaning of Life*, due to be published in 2011.

For a vivid account of the impact and comfort of a child's imaginary friend, see the story of the young girl with "the little purple man" in Richard Dawkins' *The God Delusion* (New York: Houghton Mifflin, 2006), 349.

Chapter 5

This book elaborates the by-product theory of religious belief. There is another theory that religious belief is a separate, ingrained aspect of human nature and the product of group-selection processes. A reader interested in pursuing this view should look at David Sloan Wilson's *Darwin's Cathedral: Evolution, Religion and the Nature of Society* (Chicago: University of Chicago Press, 2002) and Nicholas Wade's *Faith Instinct: How Religion Evolved and Why It Endures* (New York: Penguin Press, 2009). For anyone interested in the group-selected adaptation vs. by-product debate, see Richard Sosis's paper, "The Adaptationist-Byproduct Debate on the Evolution of Religion: Five Misunderstandings of the Adaptationist Program," *Journal of Cognition and Culture* 9 (2009): 315–332. For yet an entirely behavioral view of religion, see Lyle Steadman and Craig Palmer's *The Supernatural and Natural Selection: The Evolution of Religion* (Boulder, CO: Paradigm Publishers, 2008).

Decoupled cognition's importance to religion is well outlined in Pascal Boyer's *Religion Explained: The Evolutionary Origin of Religious Belief* (New York: Basic Books, 2001).

Robert Dunbar's explanation of religion's use of intensionality is found in "We Believe," *New Scientist* 189 (2006): 30–33.

The theory that we are born altruists and then develop strategic self-interest is Michael Tomasello's, the developmental psychologist who codirects the Max Planck Institute of Evolutionary Anthropology in Leipzig, Germany. The institute's experiments with young children and chimpanzees that tease out the inborn capacities for cooperation and understanding others' goals are wonderful to watch. Tomasello and his group have numerous articles, and he has a book titled *Why We Cooperate* (Cambridge, MA: MIT Press, 2009). The idea of language growing out of shared intentions is fully developed in Tomasello's *Origins of Human Communication* (Cambridge, MA: MIT Press, 2010).

The comic movie actor Sacha Baron-Cohen has a cousin, Simon Baron-Cohen, a psychologist at Cambridge University, who has significantly advanced our understanding of Asperger's syndrome and autism spectrum illnesses. He sees male brains as oriented toward systemizing and female brains toward empathizing. Theory-of-mind capacities in women are on average superior to men's. The autism spectrum illnesses represent the extreme male brain. He has numerous scientific papers and an accessible book for the interested general reader, *The Essential Difference: Male and Female Brains and the Truth about Autism* (New York: Basic Books, 2003). The ability to empathize is often hard for men to develop. Studies showed long ago the importance for even premature infants to see faces.

The description of transference as a normal psychological mechanism of the mind is in Randolph Nesse and Alan Lloyd's chapter on evolved psychological defenses, "The Evolution of Psychodynamic Mechanisms," in *The Adapted*

Mind: Evolutionary Psychology and the Generation of Culture, ed. Jerome Barkow, Leda Cosmides, and John Tooby (New York: Oxford University Press, 1992).

Chapter 6

The term "hyperactive agency detection device" comes from the work of Justin Barrett's *Why Would Anyone Believe in God?* (Lanham, MD: AltaMira Press, 2004). This is a marvelous little book that clearly describes many of the cognitive mechanisms used in religion, but it is marred by the unexpected, unexplained, and inexplicable confession of Christian faith in one of the last paragraphs. The importance of our vulnerability to anthropomorphize religion is the basis of Stuart Guthrie's book, *Faces in the Cloud: A New Theory of Religion* (New York: Oxford University Press, 1993). Richard Coss, a professor of psychology at the University of California at Davis, introduced to me the idea and evidence for the persistence in our minds of mechanisms from our australopithicene ancestors.

Our quirk to construct minimally counterintuitive worlds is the bedrock of the cognitive neuroscience of religious belief. This is detailed in Pascal Boyer's *Religion Explained: The Evolutionary Origin of Religious Belief* (New York: Basic Books, 2001) and Scott Atran's *In Gods We Trust: The Evolutionary Landscape of Religion* (New York: Oxford University Press 2002). Why do we all know the story of Little Red Riding Hood? It contains two minimally counterintuitive occurrences, the talking wolf and then the little girl and the grandmother emerging alive from the wolf's belly.

We remember minimally counterintuitive ideas better than regular intuitive ideas or bizarre ideas. For empirical evidence of this, see "Memory and Mystery: The Cultural Selection of Minimally Counterintuitive Narratives" by Ara Norenzayan, Scott Atran, Jason Faulkner and Mark Schaller in *Cognitive Science* 30 (2006): 531–553. This article demonstrates how minimally counterintuitive elements are central to successful folk tales and religious narratives. The supernatural elements remain connected to the everyday and can relieve core existential human problems that are rationally intractable, such as death. They can be easily remembered, repeated, and handed down to the next generation.

An accessible book that outlines the cognitive neuroscience of religion in more detail than ours is Todd Tremlin's *Minds and Gods: The Cognitive Foundations of Religion* (New York: Oxford University Press, 2006).

In one of the most important forewords to any book, Robert Trivers introduced the concept of self-deception in the original 1976 edition of Richard Dawkins' *The Selfish Gene* and it can be found in the book's thirtieth anniversary edition. The notion of intuitive theists and promiscuous teleology was introduced by Deborah Kelemen, "Are Children Intuitive Theists? Reasoning about Purpose and Design in Nature," *Psychological Sciences* 15 (2004): 295–301. Robin Cornwell pointed out the extension to the idea that there are only atheists in foxholes. The religious buy health insurance, use car seats for their infants, and expect others to also behave as if there is no divine protection in this life. If you are in the military or know someone who is, consider Military Association of Atheists and Freethinkers, www.maaf.info.

Our difficulty understanding evolution is nicely captured in Daniel Dennett's lecture "Human Nature and Belief," Darwin Festival, Cambridge University, July 8, 2009. It can be easily accessed with a Google search. He uses the analogy of computers, which can do complex calculations with no understanding of mathematics. We are unfamiliar with competence without comprehension. Natural selection gives us beautiful designs with no skilled designer, reasons without a reasoner. The ability to comprehend is a recent outcome of the evolutionary process.

The "Eye of God" image seems to have a life of its own as a religious figure. Beginning in 2003 and reappearing sporadically after that, the image "went viral" via e-mail chains, as noted on the Internet hoax–debunking Web site Snopes.com.

One such e-mail, noted on the site, reads: "This photo is a very rare one, taken by NASA. It is called the Eye of God. This kind of event occurs once in 3000 years. This photo has done miracles in many lives. Make a wish. . . . you have looked into the eye of God. Surely you will see changes in your life within a day. Whether you believe it or not, don't keep this e-mail with you. Pass this to at least 7 persons."

According to Snopes.com, "the photo is a real image of the Helix nebula, although it's technically not a single photo but a composite image taken by NASA's orbiting Hubble telescope and a land based telescope." The Web site continues, "The Helix nebula does not naturally appear with the colors shown. . . . [T]he tinting of the image is artificial. The picture's "eye of god" appellation is a title coined by an admirer of the photo . . . not something designated by NASA, and the nebula is also visible all the time, not merely 'once in three thousand years.'"

The spontaneous designation of an artificially enhanced composite photograph of a nebula as the eye of a deity powerfully illustrates humankind's need and ability to create gods.

Chapter 7

A quick search of the Web will bring any interested reader full descriptions of Stanley Milgram's work and even videos of recent experiments that replicate his findings.

There has been a revolution in the psychology and cognitive neuroscience of morality. One of the best places to start to learn about this subject is Jonathan Haidt's home page and his many writings on morality. "Morality: A Comprehensive Review of Moral Psychology," a chapter he wrote for the *Handbook of Social Psychology*, is a superb overview that will bring an interested reader to the current debates. For a concise view of his synthesis, read Haidt's "The New Synthesis in Moral Psychology," *Science* 316 (2007): 998–1002.

For an enthralling discussion of animal morality, see Marc Bekoff and Jessica Pierce, *Wild Justice: The Moral Lives of Animals* (Chicago: University of Chicago Press, 2009).

The old notion that science and scientists have nothing to say about morality and moral values is turned on its head by one of my heroes, Sam Harris. In his latest book, *The Moral Landscape: How Science Can Determine Human Values* (New York: Free Press, 2010), he argues that science, scientists, and neuroscience are central to shaping human morality in all its dimensions.

The work with young children by Paul Bloom and his group at Yale is simply marvelous. See his book titled *Descartes' Baby: How the Science of Child Development Explains What Makes Us Human* (New York: Basic Books, 2004). Their ingenious experiments, which tease out moral inferential systems in children as young as three months old, are psychological science at its best. For a fun introduction see Bloom's article titled "The Moral Life of Babies," *New York Times Magazine*, May 5, 2010. Robert Sapolsky, the Stanford neuroscientist, has an enjoyable essay in the November 14, 2010, *New York Times*, "This Is Your Brain on Metaphors," which lays out how our moral emotions are based on ancient animal reactions. The same area of our brain lights up whether we are eating fetid food, smelling awful food, thinking about disgusting food, or thinking about some scumbag who has robbed a widow.

The dynamics of suicide terrorism and particularly the importance of kin psychology to recruitment can be found in Scott Atran's outstanding "Genesis of Suicide Terrorism," *Science* 299 (2003): 1534–1539.

Richard Sosis describes the importance of costly signaling to religious ritual in "The Adaptative Value of Religious Ritual," *American Scientist* 92 (2004): 166–172.

Chapter 8
Barbara Ehrenreich's book *Dancing in the Streets: A History of*

Collective Joy (New York: Henry Holt, 2006) is an informative delight. She thinks one of the original functions of dancing was to scare away predators at night. A provocative comment is her observation that we have many cave paintings of groups in dance and ritual, yet we have no early paintings of just two people talking together.

One of my favorite neuroscientists is Barry Jacobs in the psychology department at Princeton University. A nice introduction to serotonin is his "Serotonin, Motor Activity and Depression-Related Disorders," *American Scientist* 82 (1994): 456–463. For a curious reader, Stephen Stahl's books are a superb introduction to neurochemistry and psychopharmacology. They are set up so the reader can key off the illustrations, which begin at the fundamentals of neurochemistry and take you through the drugs used to treat the mind. *Stahl's Essential Psychopharmacology: Neuroscientific Basis and Practical Applications*, 3rd ed. (New York: Cambridge University Press, 2008).

The recent work that demonstrated how religious priming increased punishment of unfair behavior was done by Ryan McKay, Charles Efferson, Harvey Whitehouse, and Ernst Fehr, "Wrath of God: Religious Primes and Punishment," *Proceedings of the Royal Society B*, November 24, 2010, http://rspb.royalsocietypublishing.org/content/early/2010/11/17/rspb.2010.2125.abstract?papetoc.

Maurice Apprey, a psychoanalyst born and raised in Africa, told us the following story: "Mr. Coleman, the headmaster of our Methodist church in Saltpond, Ghana, West

Africa, was also our organist. With consternation and in horror, he approached and chided my Methodist middle school classmates during recess for chanting and encircling a tree with the following admonition: 'Stop boys! Don't you know that this is just how gods are created!?' The boys were stunned, intrigued, and amused at the same time by the real potential that they could create a god through a game around a tree."

Rodney Needham, "Percussion and Transition," *Man* 2 (1967): 606–614.

Nicholas Wade, in *The Faith Instinct: How Religion Evolved and Why It Endures* (New York: Penguin Press, 2009), discusses the similarity between the three religions of the Kung San, the Andaman Islanders, and the Australian aborigines as well as their close common origin to our earliest ancestors in Africa. Although I disagree with his view that religion is a group-selected adaptation, I am indebted to him. Reading his description of their religions based on song, dance, and trance triggered the link between the earliest religion and how our ancestors harnessed our neurochemistry to cement religions into their brains.

Robin Dunbar's "We Believe," *New Scientist* 189 (2006): 30–33, pointed out the relationship of endorphins to the physically stressful nature of most religious rituals. My view is a broader attempt to link endorphins, oxytocin, and the monoamine neurotransmitters to the origins of religion.

Daniel Dennett's review of Walter Burkett's *Creation of the Sacred: Tracks of Biology in Early Religions* titled "Appraising Grace: What Evolutionary Good is God?"

Sciences (January–February 1997): 39–44, has an excellent description of the mere-messenger strategy.

For the debate about music as by-product or sexually selected adaptation, see Pinker's *How the Mind Works*, Geoffrey Miller's *The Mating Mind: How Sexual Choice Shaped the Evolution of Human Nature* (New York: Doubleday, 2000), and Daniel Levitin's *This Is Your Brain On Music: The Science of a Human Obsession* (New York: Dutton, 2006).

Scott Wiltermuth and Chip Heath published interesting experiments about synchrony and cooperation in which subjects do not have to do heavy physical exercise to increase cooperative feelings; they just have to move in synchrony. See "Synchrony and Cooperation," *Psychological Science* 20 (2009): 1–5. Robin Dunbar's group devised the experiment with rowers that shows group effort, with work output controlled, raises endorphins and pain thresholds. Emma E. A. Cohen, Robin Ejsmond-Frey, Nicola Knight, and R. I. M. Dunbar, "Rowers' High: Behavioral Synchrony Is Correlated with Elevated Pain Thresholds," *Biology Letters*, 2009, http://rsbl.royalsocietypublishing.org/content/6/1/106.full.

It was a fellow University of Virginia faculty member, James Coan, who did the ingenious experiment in which women have brain scans under a threat scenario, successively not holding hands, holding the hand of a stranger, and holding the hand of a partner. James A. Coan, Hillary S. Schaefer, and Richard J. Davidson, "Lending a Hand: Social Regulation of the Neural Response to Treat," *Psychological Science* 17 (2006): 1032–1039. Benedict Carey wrote a lovely piece in the

New York Times on February 22, 2010, "Evidence that Little Touches Do Mean So Much," that summarizes some of the research on touch and its impact.

I have had the privilege of working with anthropologist Helen Fisher, whose research has dissected the neuroanatomy of love. Our work on the sexual side effects of serotonin-enhancing antidepressants summarizes the neurobiology of sexual desire and romantic love, "Lust, Romance, Attachment: Do the Sexual Side Effects of Serotonin-Enhancing Antidepressants Jeopardize Romantic Love, Marriage, and Fertility?" *Evolutionary Cognitive Neuroscience*, ed. Steven Platek (Cambridge, MA: MIT Press 2006).

The late Sheikh Yassin's comments about women suicide bombers can be seen in Barbara Victor's documentary, *Women Suicide Bombers*, available on her Web site, and are in her book, *Army of Roses: Inside the World of Palestinian Women Suicide Bombers* (Emmaus, PA: Rodale, 2003).

My friend Robin Cornwell notes that monks are also "brides of Christ"—set apart exclusively to his love. Another marriage image is of Christ as bridegroom of the church. In the Song of Songs, the marriage imagery is said to be of God's love for Israel and, of course, the marital love between two flesh and blood people. Every Christian is in some sense the bride of Christ. Even men may qualify. Christianity would appear to have sanctioned gay marriage for a very long time.

The concept of parental investment was elaborated by the brilliant biologist Robert Trivers, already noted here for his concept of self-deception, in "Parental Investment and Sexual

Selection," in *Sexual Selection and the Descent of Man, 1871–1971*, ed. Bernard Campbell, 136–179 (Chicago, IL: Aldine, 1972).

To learn about about Julia Sweeney's play, now available on DVD, see www.juliasweeney.com/letting_go_mini/.

Despite religion's oppression of women, why do they often endure and pass on the bondage of faith? See Robin Cornwell's "Why Women Are Bound to Religion: An Evolutionary Perspective," http://richarddawkins.net/articles/3609.

The 2009 study of Arizona college students showing that religious feelings increased as a part of sexual competition between same sexes was done by Douglas Kenrick's group. Yexin J. Li, Adam B. Cohen, Jason Weeden, and Douglas T. Kenrick, "Mating Competitors Increase Religious Beliefs," *Journal of Experimental Social Psychology* 46 (2010): 428–431.

Chapter 9

Lone Frank, the Danish neurobiologist and journalist, has an underappreciated book titled *Mindfield: How Brain Science Is Changing Our World* (Oxford: One World Publications, 2009). Her excellent chapter on the cognitive neuroscience of religion contains a vivid description of her visit to Michael Persinger's laboratory and her own experience in the "God Helmet."

My discussion of Michael Persinger and Andrew Newberg is taken from L. S. St-Pierre and Michael A. Persinger, "Experimental Facilitation of the Sensed Presence Is Predicted by Specific Patterns of Applied Magnetic Fields Not by Suggestibility: Re-analyses of 19 Experiments," *International Journal of Neuroscience* 116 (2006): 1079–1096; Michael A.

Persinger, "Are Our Brains Structured to Avoid Refutations of the Belief in God? An Experimental Study," *Religion* 39 (2009): 34–42; Andrew Newberg and Mark Robert Waldman, *How God Changes Your Brain* (New York: Random House, 2009); *Sharon Begley*, "Religion and the Brain," *Newsweek*, May 7, 2001; Jack Hitt, "This Is Your Brain on God," *Wired* 7, no. 11 (November 1999); and Constance Holden, "Tongues on the Mind," *Science NOW*, November 2, 2006.

At the end of his 2009 article, Dr. Persinger reminds us, "That a belief in 'some type' of God must have adaptive utility has never been examined by the scientific method. The frequent presumption that affiliation with one of the myriad of religious organizations, each purporting to exclusively access the validity of this belief, is beneficial for humanity has never been verified. Human history has been replete with cases of peoples being marginalized, excluded, subjugated, or killed simply because they did not believe in the same God. Until the neurocognitive processes and multiple neuro-anatomical pathways can be isolated, understood, and controlled, the God belief should be considered the source of potentially dangerous human behaviors."

Kapogiannis and colleagues' neuroimaging study of ordinary believers and nonbelievers is, Dimitrios Kapogiannis, Aron K. Barbey, Michael Su, Giovanna Zamboni, Frank Krueger, and Jordan Grafman, "Cognitive and Neural Foundations of Religious Belief," *Proceedings of the National Academy of Science* 106 (2009): 4876–4881. The study is a triumph of science over politics. It comes from the National

Institutes of Health during the last years of the conservative and religious George W. Bush administration. One wonders if it would have been published had the 2008 presidential election had a different outcome.

Sam Harris, whose books *The End of Faith*, *Letter to a Christian Nation*, and *The Moral Landscape* have garnered him much deserved attention as an articulate foe of religion, is also a neuroscientist. His neural imaging work on believers and nonbelievers was published in 2009. Sam Harris, Jonas T. Kaplan, Ashley Curiel, Susan Y. Bookheimer, Marco Jacoboni, and Mark S. Cohen, "The Neural Correlates of Religious and Nonreligious Belief," *PLoS One* 4, no. 10: e7272.

Environment, piety, and parasites: Two other interesting scientific works have added to the literature about religion and religion's effect on humanity in ways that may not have previously been considered. In a 2005 look at raw cross-cultural anthropologic data, Robert M. Sapolsky, a Stanford professor of biology and neurology, extracted information showing that religious ideas actually can be shaped by geography and ecology. Historically, rain forest dwellers, with nature's abundance all around, tended to be polytheists, believing in spirits based on nature and less likely to assume that gods intervene in their lives. Desert dwellers, living in a monotonous, harsh, and unforgiving environment, were more likely to believe in a single, sometimes harsh, misogynistic, interventionist god. For various reasons, it was the god of the desert dwellers that was passed on to much of humanity. See his *Monkeyluv: And Other Essays on Our Lives as Animals* (New York: Scribner, 2005).

A 2008 study at the University of New Mexico has demonstrated that infectious disease, specifically organisms that are transmitted between humans as opposed to those they catch from animals, influence people's religiosity. In short, religion can be hazardous to health. Why? Religions promote collectivism—me and mine against you and yours. Those areas of the world that have the highest burden of human-to-human infectious disease are the most religious. Corey L. Fincher and Randy Thornhill, "Assortative Sociality, Limited Dispersal, Infectious Disease and the Genesis of the Global Pattern of Religion Diversity," *Proceedings of the Royal Society B* 275 (2008): 2587–2594.

That our brains are ethical by design comes from Joshua Greene's essay "Fruit Flies of the Moral Mind," in *What's Next: Dispatches on the Future of Science*, ed. Max Brockman.

Chapter 10

Matthew Chapman, Charles Darwin's great-great-grandson, wrote deeply personal accounts of the Scopes Trial, *Trials of the Monkey: An Accidental Memoir* (New York: Picador, 2000) and the Dover trial, *40 Days and 40 Nights* (New York: Harper Collins, 2007).

Kenneth Miller, the Brown University biologist and textbook author, testified at the Dover trial:

Q. Is evolution antireligious?
A. I certainly don't think so, and I devoted a whole book to arguing why I didn't think it was.
Q. Don't some scientists invoke evolution in their arguments

to say that, in fact, science and evolution is antireligious, it's anti-God?

A. Yes, they do. And I can certainly think of any number of specific examples from distinguished evolutionary biologists like Richard Dawkins or philosophers who have written about evolution like Daniel Dennett or William Paley. But as I said earlier, it's very important to appreciate that every word that comes forth from the mouth of a scientist is not necessarily science. And every word that one says on the meaning or the importance of evolutionary theory is not necessarily scientific. Richard Dawkins, for example, has been eloquent in saying that for him, understanding that life and the origin of species has a material cause frees him from the need to believe in a divine being. I don't know if I've been as eloquent as Richard Dawkins, but I have worked very hard in my own way to say that for me, the notion that we are united in a great chain of being with every other living thing on this planet confirms my faith in a divine purpose and in a divine plan and means that when I go to church on Sunday, I thank the creator for this wonderful and bounteous earth and for the process of evolution that gave rise to such beauty and gave rise to such diversity that surrounds us. Those are my sentiments, in the same way that Dawkins' are his. But I'm not speaking scientifically, and I'm not speaking as a scientist, and that's, I think, the critical distinction.

Q. So you wrote a whole book exploring this intersection between science and faith?

A. That's correct. . . . Now, I believe in that very strongly, but I certainly recognize that my views on this are not science and they are not scientific. My coauthor, Joseph

Levine, who also is a religious person, I have to tell you, has different views of faith, belongs to a different faith, and follows a different religious tradition than I do. Joe and I both have enormous respect for religion. We both believe that the evolutionary theory is fully compatible with our different religious beliefs, but we also recognize that our religious beliefs are not scientific, that they are philosophical, theological, and deeply personal, and, as such, they don't belong in a science curriculum, and they certainly don't belong in a science textbook.

Judge John E. Jones III concludes in his decision in *Kitzmiller v. Dover Area School District*, "Both Defendants and many of the leading proponents of ID [intelligent design] make a bedrock assumption which is utterly false. Their presupposition is that evolutionary theory is antithetical to a belief in the existence of a supreme being and to religion in general. Repeatedly in this trial, Plaintiffs' scientific experts testified that the theory of evolution represents good science, is overwhelmingly accepted by the scientific community, and that it in no way conflicts with, nor does it deny, the existence of a divine creator."

Jerry Coyne's pithy summary of the distinction between science and religion, "In religion faith is a virtue; in science it's a vice," comes from "Science and Religion Aren't Friends," a column in the October 11, 2010, edition of *USA Today*.

Fundamentalists of all stripes advocate murder, misogyny, the suspension of civil liberties, prohibitions on life-saving medical research, and early "godly" education that amounts to child abuse. Will the world ever awaken from its long nightmare of religious belief? Christian fundamentalists, jihadists, creationists, and "intelligent design" theorists all use modern electronic devices, yet they choose to ignore that the same science that dictates the flow of electrons in cell phones and computers reveals how the universe really works. Modern electronics is part of the same science that confirms natural selection and reveals our origins and evolutionary history from primates, monkeys, apes, and early hominids. It leaves no room for divine intervention, a 6,000-year-old earth, or a world built in a week by a divine architect and construction engineer. Tim Folger, foreword to *The Best American Science and Nature Writing 2004* (New York: Houghton Mifflin, 2004).

Authors' Note

If this little book has interested you in the new debates about religion, you will enjoy any and all of the following:

www.richarddawkins.net
Ayaan Hirsi Ali, *Infidel* (2007)
      and *Nomad* (2010)
Richard Dawkins, *The God Delusion* (2006)
Daniel Dennett, *Breaking the Spell* (2006)
Sam Harris, *The End of Faith* (2004),
      Letter to a Christian Nation (2006),
      and *The Moral Landscape* (2010)
Christopher Hitchens, *God Is Not Great* (2007)
      and *The Portable Atheist* (2007)

Glossary

The following are the principal mechanisms of our minds that combine to give us religious belief.

attachment. This most basic of human needs almost defines religion's premise. Religion supplements or supplants family.

childhood credulity. We all believe too readily, with too little evidence. Children are even more vulnerable, especially when taught by someone with a mantle of authority.

costly signaling. A man whipping his back to a pulp must be committed to his faith and will be my ally if I too believe.

decoupled cognition. This allows us to conduct a complex social interaction in our mind with an unseen other.

deference to authority. We are all more deferential to authority figures than we can see or want to admit to ourselves.

dreams. They are perhaps the original perception interpreted as proof of another world of people and ancestors.

hyperactive agency detection. This leads us to assume that unknown forces are human agents. It evolved to protect us. We mistake a shadow for a burglar and never mistake a burglar for a shadow. It encourages anthropomorphism.

kin psychology. We are hardwired to prefer our kin over others.

intensionality. This allows us to speculate about others' thoughts about our thoughts, desires, beliefs, and intentions.

intuitive reasoning. This helps us "fill in the blanks" of logic.

mind-body dualism. This allows us to separate mind from body and to believe in a "soul."

minimally counterintuitive worlds. This allows belief in the supernatural, as long as it's not too "super" and does not violate too many basic tenets of humanness.

mirror neurons. We literally feel each other's pain; this is inborn, not invented by religion. We are born caring about others.

moral-feeling systems. These generate our moral decisions. They are instinctual and automatic. Because they operate largely outside of awareness, religions can claim ownership of them and insist we are only moral with faith.

precautionary reasoning. Better safe than sorry.

promiscuous teleology. This arises from our bias to understand the world as purpose driven.

reciprocal altruism. You scratch my back. I'll scratch yours.

ritual behavior. This enhances group cohesion and tests who is committed to the group.

romantic love. People fall in love with Jesus, or whichever deity figure they choose, calling on the same mental capacities that lead them to attachment.

song and dance. They harness our neurochemistry that reduces pain and fear and increases trust, love, self-esteem, and cooperation.

theory of mind. This allows us to "read" others' possible thoughts, desires, beliefs, and intentions.

transference. We can accept religious figures as easily as we accepted the family figures we've known since birth. We transfer our familial thoughts to religious figures.